PASTA

Pasta is versatile, economical and best of all good for you. The ways it can be served and the forms it comes in are almost limitless as the recipes in this book show you. Most of the recipes are quick and easy to prepare, making them ideal for weekday meals. Whether it's a substantial main meal, a quick lunch or a hearty winter soup that you are looking for, you are sure to find a recipe to suit the occasion.

CONTENTS

THE PANTRY SHELF
Unless otherwise stated the following ingredients used in this book are:

Cream Double, suitable for whipping
Flour White flour, plain or standard
Sugar White sugar

WHAT'S IN A TABLESPOON?
NEW ZEALAND
1 tablespoon =
15 mL OR 3 teaspoons
UNITED KINGDOM
1 tablespoon =
15 mL OR 3 teaspoons
AUSTRALIA
1 tablespoon =
20 mL OR 4 teaspoons
The recipes in this book were tested in Australia where a 20 mL tablespoon is standard. All measures are level.

The tablespoon in the New Zealand and United Kingdom sets of measuring spoons is 15 mL. In many recipes this difference will not matter. For recipes using baking powder, gelatine, bicarbonate of soda, small quantities of flour and cornflour, simply add another teaspoon for each tablespoon specified.

SOUPS

Soups made with pasta are hearty, healthy and satisfying. While any type of pasta can be used in soup, the smaller shapes are the most popular. A good way to use odds and ends of pasta you may have in the cupboard is to add them to soup.

Spaghetti Basil Soup

Minestrone

Italian Chicken Soup

Spinach Soup

Vermicelli Onion Soup

Chilli Chicken Soup

Italian Bean Soup

Spaghetti Basil Soup

SPAGHETTI BASIL SOUP

155 g/5 oz spaghetti, broken into pieces
2 tablespoons vegetable oil
1 onion, chopped
2 cloves garlic, crushed
60 g/2 oz slivered almonds
4 cups/1 litre/1³/4 pt chicken stock
30 g/1 oz fresh basil leaves, shredded
freshly ground black pepper

1   Cook spaghetti in boiling water in a large saucepan following packet directions. Drain and set aside.

2   Heat oil in a large saucepan and cook onion, garlic and almonds, stirring over a medium heat for 6-7 minutes or until onions are transparent.

3   Add stock and basil to pan and bring to the boil, reduce heat, cover and simmer for 10 minutes. Stir in spaghetti and season to taste with black pepper. Spoon soup into bowls and serve immediately.

Serves 4

Sprinkled with Parmesan cheese and served with bread rolls this soup makes a wonderful summer lunch dish. Basil gives it its distinctive flavour.

MINESTRONE

315 g/10 oz dried white beans
6 cups/1.5 litres/2¹/2 pt water
6 cups/1.5 litres/2¹/2 pt chicken stock
125 g/4 oz mushrooms, sliced
155 g/5 oz green beans, chopped
2 carrots, chopped
2 zucchini (courgettes) sliced
1 leek, sliced
155 g/5 oz small shell pasta
440 g/14 oz canned tomatoes, undrained and mashed
freshly ground black pepper
grated Parmesan cheese

1   Place dried beans and 4 cups/1 litre/1³/4 pt water in a large bowl, cover and set aside to soak for 8 hours or overnight.

2   Drain beans and rinse in cold water. Place beans and stock in a large saucepan, bring to the boil and boil for 10 minutes, then reduce heat, cover and simmer for 1 hour or until beans are tender.

3   Add mushrooms, green beans, carrots, zucchini (courgettes), leek and remaining 2 cups/500 mL/16 fl oz water to pan. Bring to the boil, then reduce heat, cover and simmer for 30 minutes. Stir pasta and tomatoes into soup and cook for 10 minutes longer or until pasta is tender. Season to taste with black pepper. Sprinkle with Parmesan cheese and serve immediately.

Serves 6 as a main meal

Served with crusty bread and a glass of wine, Minestrone is a meal in itself.

Italian Chicken Soup

ITALIAN CHICKEN SOUP

12 cups/3 litres/5 pt chicken stock
4 chicken breast fillets, skinned
1 teaspoon whole black peppercorns
4 bay leaves
1 sprig fresh rosemary
1 onion, chopped
1 red pepper, chopped
2 carrots, chopped
185 g/6 oz short pasta shapes,
such as macaroni
250 g/8 oz cabbage, shredded
2 tablespoons grated Parmesan cheese

1   Place stock in a large saucepan and bring to the boil. Add chicken breasts, peppercorns, bay leaves and rosemary. Reduce heat, cover and simmer for 20 minutes or until chicken is just cooked.

2   Using a slotted spoon, remove chicken from pan and set aside to drain. Strain stock and return liquid to a clean saucepan. Add onion, red pepper, carrots and pasta to stock, cover, then bring to simmering and simmer for 20 minutes or until pasta is cooked and vegetables are tender.

3   Slice chicken. Stir chicken and cabbage into soup and cook for 5 minutes longer. Just prior to serving, stir in Parmesan cheese.

Serves 6

This clear chicken broth made with fresh chicken and vegetables makes a nutritious and delicious light meal that any weight watcher will love.

4

SPINACH SOUP

4 cups/1 litre/1³/4 pt chicken stock
60 g/2 oz small pasta shapes
250 g/8 oz frozen chopped spinach,
thawed
freshly ground black pepper
2 egg yolks

1   Place stock in a large saucepan and bring to the boil. Add pasta and spinach and cook, stirring occasionally, for 10 minutes or until pasta is tender. Season to taste with black pepper.

2   Place egg yolks in a small bowl and whisk to combine. Whisk a little hot soup into egg yolks, then stir egg yolk mixture into soup. Serve immediately.

Serves 6

VERMICELLI ONION SOUP

60 g/2 oz butter
3 onions, thinly sliced
1 tablespoon flour
1¹/4 cups/315 mL/10 fl oz hot
chicken stock
4 cups/1 litre/1³/4 pt milk
60 g/2 oz vermicelli, broken into pieces
freshly ground black pepper

1   Melt butter in a large saucepan and cook onions, stirring, over a medium heat for 6-7 minutes or until soft. Stir in flour, then gradually stir in hot stock. Cook, stirring constantly, for 4-5 minutes or until soup is smooth and thickened.

2   Stir in milk and bring to the boil. Add vermicelli and season to taste with black pepper. Cook, stirring frequently, for 8-10 minutes or until vermicelli is tender.

Serves 6

Vermicelli Onion Soup

CHILLI CHICKEN SOUP

100 g/3^1/$_2$ oz fresh egg noodles
2 tablespoons peanut oil
2 onions, chopped
2 cloves garlic, crushed
1 red chilli, finely sliced
1 teaspoon curry paste (vindaloo)
^{1}/$_4$ teaspoon ground turmeric
1 tablespoon finely chopped
fresh lemon grass or 1 tablespoon
finely grated lemon rind
4 cups/1 litre/1^3/$_4$ pt coconut milk
1^1/$_2$ cups/375 mL/12 fl oz chicken stock
375 g/12 oz cooked chicken, chopped
3 spinach leaves, finely shredded

1   Cook noodles in a large saucepan of boiling water for 3-4 minutes or until tender. Drain, then rinse noodles under cold running water. Drain again and place in individual bowls.

2   Heat oil in a large saucepan and cook onions for 2-3 minutes or until golden. Stir in garlic, chilli, curry paste, turmeric and lemon grass, and cook for 1 minute.

3   Combine coconut milk and chicken stock. Add coconut milk mixture, chicken and spinach to pan. Bring to simmering and simmer for 3-4 minutes. Spoon soup over noodles in bowls and serve immediately.

Serves 6

Coconut milk can be purchased canned, or as a long-life product in cartons, or as a powder to which you add water. These products have a short life once opened and should be used within a day or so.

Chilli Chicken Soup

You can make coconut milk using desiccated coconut and water. To make, place 500 g/1 lb desiccated coconut in a bowl and pour over 3 cups/750 mL/1^1/$_2$ pt of boiling water. Leave to stand for 30 minutes, then strain, squeezing the coconut to extract as much liquid as possible. This will make a thick coconut milk. The coconut can be used again to make a weaker coconut milk.

Italian Bean Soup

ITALIAN BEAN SOUP

1 tablespoon olive oil
2 onions, chopped
2 cloves garlic, crushed
1 red pepper, chopped
6 cups/1.5 litres/2$^{1}/_{2}$ pt chicken or
vegetable stock
125 g/4 oz small pasta shapes
$^{1}/_{2}$ cup/125 mL/4 fl oz red wine
440 g/14 oz canned tomatoes, undrained
and mashed
2 tablespoons tomato paste (purée)
315 g/10 oz canned red kidney beans,
drained
freshly ground black pepper

1 Heat oil in a large saucepan and cook onions, garlic and red pepper for 4-5 minutes or until onion softens.

2 Stir in stock, pasta, wine, tomatoes, tomato paste (purée) and beans. Bring to the boil, then reduce heat and simmer for 15 minutes. Season to taste with black pepper.

Serves 6

Thick soups made with pulses and pasta are true peasant food. But they are just as good for filling hungry teenagers.

STARTERS

*Pasta makes a light and appetising first course, but
remember not to serve too much or you will not be able to
eat the rest of your meal. For a starter, allow about 75 g/2^1/2 oz
per serve. These recipes also make great light meals, just
increase the serving size and add a salad.*

Caviar Fettuccine

Blue Cheese Penne

Fusilli with
Rosemary Sauce

Fettuccine with
Coriander

Garlic Spaghetti
with Watercress

Tomato Pasta Rolls

Spaghetti and Pesto

Smoked Salmon
Fettuccine

Chicken and Leek
Rolls

Caviar Fettuccine

8

CAVIAR FETTUCCINE

300 g/9¹/₂ oz fettuccine
2 tablespoons olive oil
2 cloves garlic, crushed
2 tablespoons finely snipped fresh chives
3 tablespoons red caviar
3 tablespoons black caviar
2 hard-boiled eggs, chopped
4 tablespoons sour cream

1   Cook fettuccine in boiling water in a large saucepan following packet directions. Drain, set aside and keep warm.

2   Heat oil in a large frying pan and cook garlic over a low heat for 3-4 minutes. Add fettuccine, chives, red and black caviar, and eggs to pan. Toss to combine. Serve immediately, topped with sour cream.

Serves 4

A truly elegant starter. This colourful dish only takes minutes to prepare and is sure to be a hit at any dinner party.
If your budget does not run to caviar, this recipe is also delicious made with red and black lumpfish roe.

BLUE CHEESE PENNE

500 g/1 lb penne

BLUE CHEESE SAUCE
1 cup/250 mL/8 fl oz cream (double)
185 g/6 oz blue cheese, crumbled
3 tablespoons grated fresh Parmesan cheese
freshly ground black pepper

1   Cook penne in boiling water in a large saucepan following packet directions. Drain, set aside and keep warm.

2   To make sauce, place cream and blue cheese in a saucepan, bring to the boil, stirring constantly, over a medium heat. As soon as the mixture reaches the boil, remove from heat and pour over pasta. Sprinkle with Parmesan cheese, season to taste with black pepper and toss to combine. Serve immediately.

Serves 6

This recipe is also wonderful using macaroni or bow pasta in place of the penne.

FUSILLI WITH ROSEMARY SAUCE

500 g fusilli or spiral pasta
1 tablespoon olive oil
2 cloves garlic, crushed
2 teaspoons finely chopped fresh rosemary or 1 teaspoon dried rosemary
440 g/14 oz canned tomatoes, drained and mashed
freshly ground black pepper
60 g/2 oz grated mozzarella cheese

1   Cook pasta in boiling water in a large saucepan following packet directions. Drain, set aside and keep warm.

2   Heat oil in a frying pan and cook garlic and rosemary, over a low heat, for 2-3 minutes. Add tomatoes, bring to simmering and simmer for 3-4 minutes. Season to taste with black pepper. Add pasta to tomato sauce and toss to combine. Serve immediately, topped with mozzarella cheese.

Serves 6

A native of the Mediterranean shores, rosemary is an extremely aromatic herb, much used by Italian cooks. It is easy to grow, but requires a sunny protected position with good drainage. In cold climates rosemary is best cultivated in a container so that it can be moved to the protection of a glasshouse in winter.

FETTUCCINE WITH CORIANDER SAUCE

500 g/1 lb fettuccine

CORIANDER SAUCE
2 cloves garlic, chopped
60 g/2 oz walnut pieces
60 g/2 oz fresh coriander leaves
15 g/^{1}/$_2$ oz fresh parsley leaves
4 tablespoons vegetable oil
60 g/2 oz grated Parmesan cheese
freshly ground black pepper

1   Cook fettuccine in boiling water in a large saucepan following packet directions. Drain, set aside and keep warm.

2   To make sauce, place garlic, walnuts, coriander and parsley in a food processor or blender and process to finely chop. With machine running, add oil in a steady stream. Add Parmesan cheese and black pepper to taste, and process to combine.

3   Spoon sauce over pasta and toss to combine. Serve immediately.

Serves 6

Coriander, a member of the carrot family, is indigenous to the Mediterranean. Also known as cilantro and Chinese parsley, it has a fresh taste and is popular in Indian, Asian, Mexican, South American and Middle Eastern cooking.

GARLIC SPAGHETTI WITH WATERCRESS

300 g/9^1/$_2$ oz spaghetti
60 g/2 oz butter
3 cloves garlic, crushed
60 g/2 oz watercress sprigs
4 tablespoons grated Parmesan cheese
freshly ground black pepper

1   Cook spaghetti in boiling water in a large saucepan following packet directions. Drain, set aside and keep warm.

2   Melt butter in a large frying pan and cook garlic, over a low heat, for 3-4 minutes. Remove pan from heat and add spaghetti, watercress and Parmesan cheese. Season to taste with black pepper and toss to combine. Serve immediately.

Serves 4

When cooking garlic it is important to use a low heat so that the garlic does not brown or burn. Burnt garlic has an unpleasant, bitter taste.

Fettuccine with Coriander Sauce

TOMATO PASTA ROLLS

2 cups/250 g/8 oz flour
2 eggs
2 tablespoons water
2 tablespoons concentrated
tomato paste (purée)
1 tablespoon olive oil

SPINACH FILLING
500 g/1 lb frozen spinach, thawed
and well drained
375 g/12 oz ricotta or
cottage cheese
2 eggs
90 g/3 oz grated Parmesan cheese
1 teaspoon ground nutmeg
freshly ground black pepper
12 slices prosciutto or thinly sliced ham
500 g/1 lb sliced mozzarella cheese

When the menu calls for finger food, and something a little more substantial is required, these rolls are ideal. Or serve individual slices with a small green salad as a colourful first course for a dinner party. Either way, the time taken to make these will be well rewarded.

1   Place flour, eggs, water, tomato paste (purée) and oil in a food processor and process to combine. Turn dough onto a lightly floured surface and knead for 5 minutes or until dough is smooth and elastic. Wrap dough in plastic food wrap and set aside to stand for 15 minutes.

2   To make filling, place spinach, ricotta cheese, eggs, Parmesan cheese, nutmeg and black pepper to taste in a bowl, and mix to combine.

3   Divide dough in half and roll out one half to form a rectangle 30 x 45 cm/12 x 18 in. Spread with half the filling mixture, leaving a 2.5 cm/1 in border, then top with half the prosciutto or ham and half the mozzarella cheese. Fold in borders on long sides, then roll up from the short side. Wrap roll in a piece of washed calico cloth and secure ends with string. Repeat with remaining ingredients to make a second roll.

4   Half fill a baking dish with water and place on the stove top. Bring to the boil, add rolls, reduce heat, cover dish with aluminium foil or lid and simmer for 30 minutes. Turn rolls once or twice during cooking. Remove rolls from water and allow to cool for 5 minutes. Remove calico from rolls and refrigerate until firm. To serve, cut rolls into slices.

Serves 12

Tomato Pasta Rolls

SPAGHETTI AND PESTO

500 g/1 lb spaghetti

PESTO
125 g/4 oz fresh basil leaves
3 tablespoons pine nuts
4 cloves garlic, crushed
4 tablespoons olive oil
freshly ground black pepper

1   Cook spaghetti in boiling water in a large saucepan following packet directions. Drain, set aside and keep warm.

2   To make Pesto, place basil, pine nuts and garlic in a food processor or blender and process to finely chop all ingredients. With machine running, add oil in a steady steam. Season to taste with black pepper.

3   Add Pesto to spaghetti and toss to combine. Serve immediately.

Pesto is delicious served with any ribbon pasta. You might like to use fettuccine, tagliatelle or pappardelle in place of the spaghetti in this recipe. Pesto is also wonderful stirred into vegetable soups, tossed through steamed or microwaved vegetables and added to mayonnaise to make an interesting dressing for potato salad.

Spaghetti and Pesto

Serves 6

SMOKED SALMON FETTUCCINE

500 g/1 lb fettuccine

SMOKED SALMON SAUCE
125 g/4 oz fresh or frozen peas
1/4 cup/60 mL/2 fl oz white wine
1 1/4 cups/315 mL/10 fl oz cream
(double)
8 slices smoked salmon
3 spring onions, finely chopped
freshly ground black pepper

1 Cook fettuccine in boiling water in a large saucepan following packet directions. Drain, set aside and keep warm.

2 To make sauce, blanch peas in boiling water for 2 minutes. Refresh under cold running water, drain and set aside. Place wine in a large frying pan and bring to the boil. Stir in 1 cup/ 250 mL/8 fl oz cream and boil until sauce reduces and thickens. Place 4 slices smoked salmon, spring onions and remaining cream in a food processor and purée. Stir smoked salmon mixture into sauce and cook until sauce is hot.

3 Cut remaining salmon slices into strips. Add salmon strips and peas to sauce and season to taste with black pepper. Spoon sauce over fettuccine and toss to combine. Serve immediately.

Smoked Salmon Fettuccine

Serves 6

CHICKEN AND LEEK ROLLS

12 spinach lasagne sheets
2 tablespoons grated fresh
Parmesan cheese

CHICKEN AND LEEK FILLING
2 teaspoons vegetable oil
3 leeks, finely sliced
3 chicken breast fillets, cut into
thin strips
$^1/_2$ cup/125 mL/4 fl oz chicken stock
3 teaspoons cornflour blended with
2 tablespoons water
1 teaspoon French mustard
2 teaspoons chopped fresh basil
freshly ground black pepper

1   Cook lasagne sheets in boiling water in a large saucepan until tender. Drain, set aside and keep warm.

2   To make filling, heat oil in a large frying pan and cook leeks and chicken, stirring, for 4-5 minutes or until chicken is brown. Stir in stock, cornflour mixture, mustard and basil and cook, stirring, for 2 minutes longer. Season to taste with black pepper.

3   Place spoonfuls of filling on lasagne sheets, roll up, top with Parmesan cheese and serve immediately.

Serves 6

Chicken and Leek Rolls

MAIN MEALS

*Pasta is a food of our times. In recent years it has
graduated from being a humble staple to a sought-after
food. It is available in many shapes, sizes and flavours
from supermarkets, corner shops … in fact
almost anywhere that food is sold.*

Fettuccine with Leeks

500 g/1 lb fettuccine
60 g/2 oz butter
2 large leeks, halved and thinly sliced
185 g/6 oz ham, cut into strips
1 red pepper, cut into strips
1 cup/250 mL/8 fl oz cream (double)
freshly ground black pepper

1   Cook fettuccine in boiling water in a large saucepan following packet directions. Drain, set aside and keep warm.

2   Heat butter in a large frying pan and cook leeks for 8-10 minutes or until tender. Add ham and red pepper and cook for 2-3 minutes longer. Stir in cream, bring to the boil, then reduce heat and simmer for 4-5 minutes.

Serves 4

3   Add fettuccine to pan and toss to combine. Serve immediately.

Fresh or packaged dried pasta? Which is the best? Neither is superior – they are just different. Fresh pasta is more delicate and keeps for only a few days, while dried pasta is more robust and ideal for serving with heartier sauces. Dried pasta also has the advantage of being less expensive, easier to store and of having a longer life. With a packet of pasta in the house there's a meal only minutes away.

Tuna Cannelloni

2 sheets fresh tomato lasagne
4 tablespoons grated Parmesan cheese

TUNA AND MUSHROOM FILLING
1 onion, finely sliced
1 clove garlic, crushed
125 g/4 oz mushrooms, chopped
250 g/8 oz ricotta or cottage cheese
440 g/14 oz canned tuna in water, drained and $^1/_2$ cup/125 mL/4 fl oz liquid reserved
2 tablespoons finely chopped fresh dill
freshly ground black pepper

YOGURT SAUCE
15 g/$^1/_2$ oz butter
2 tablespoons flour
1 teaspoon lemon juice
1 cup/200 g/6$^1/_2$ oz natural yogurt
freshly ground black pepper

1   To make filling, place onion and garlic in a nonstick frying pan and cook, stirring, for 4-5 minutes or until onion is soft. Add mushrooms and cook, stirring, for 3-4 minutes longer. Place ricotta cheese and tuna in a bowl and mix to combine. Stir in mushroom mixture and dill. Season to taste with black pepper.

2   Cut lasagne sheets in half. Spoon filling down the centre of each half sheet and roll up. Place rolls join side down in a lightly oiled ovenproof dish.

3   To make sauce, melt butter in a small saucepan, stir in flour and cook for 1 minute. Stir in reserved tuna liquid and lemon juice and cook, stirring, for 3-4 minutes or until sauce thickens. Remove pan from heat and set aside to cool. Mix in yogurt and season to taste with black pepper. Return pan to a low heat and cook for 2-3 minutes longer.

4   Pour sauce over cannelloni and sprinkle with Parmesan cheese. Bake for 30 minutes or until heated through and top is golden.

Oven temperature
180°C, 350°F, Gas 4

Rather than making up the cannelloni from lasagne sheets, you may prefer to use purchased cannelloni tubes. Make up the filling as described in recipe and use to fill the tubes. Then place in an ovenproof dish, top with sauce and Parmesan cheese, and bake as directed in recipe.

Fettuccine with Leeks   *Serves 4*

SPAGHETTI WITH RATATOUILLE SAUCE

500 g/1 lb wholemeal spaghetti
4 tablespoons grated Parmesan cheese

RATATOUILLE SAUCE
1 eggplant (aubergine), diced
1 large onion, sliced
1 clove garlic, crushed
1 green pepper, diced
2 zucchini (courgettes), diced
500 g/1 lb tomatoes, peeled, seeded and
roughly chopped
$^1/_2$ cup/125 mL/4 fl oz dry white wine
1 tablespoon finely chopped fresh basil
$^1/_2$ teaspoon dried thyme
$^1/_2$ teaspoon dried oregano
freshly ground black pepper

1   To make sauce, place eggplant
(aubergine), onion, garlic, green pepper,
zucchini (courgettes), tomatoes, wine,
basil, thyme and oregano in a nonstick
frying pan, and cook over a low heat,
stirring occasionally, for 30-45 minutes
or until mixture forms a thick sauce.
Season to taste with black pepper.

2   Cook spaghetti in boiling water in a
large saucepan following packet
directions. Drain spaghetti, spoon sauce
over, toss to combine and sprinkle with
Parmesan cheese.

Serves 4

Use this delicious and
versatile Ratatouille Sauce as
a topping for baked
potatoes, or eat it on its own,
hot or cold. The length of
cooking time depends upon
whether you wish the texture
of the sauce to be crunchy
or very soft.

SEAFOOD FETTUCCINE

500 g/1 lb mixed coloured fettuccine

SPICY SEAFOOD SAUCE
1 tablespoon olive oil
1 onion, sliced
1 red pepper, diced
1 clove garlic, crushed
1 red chilli, seeded and finely chopped
$^1/_2$ teaspoon ground cumin
$^1/_2$ teaspoon ground coriander
440 g/14 oz canned tomatoes,
undrained and mashed
$^1/_4$ cup/60 mL/2 fl oz dry white wine
1 tablespoon tomato paste (purée)
155 g/5 oz calamari, cut into rings
155 g/5 oz cleaned fresh mussels
in shells
500 g/1 lb uncooked large prawns,
peeled and deveined
4 tablespoons finely chopped
fresh coriander
freshly ground black pepper

1   To make sauce, heat oil in a large
saucepan and cook onion, red pepper,
garlic, chilli, cumin and ground
coriander for 3-4 minutes or until onion
is soft. Add tomatoes, wine and tomato
paste (purée) and cook over a medium
heat for 30 minutes longer or until sauce
reduces and thickens.

2   Add calamari to sauce and cook for 5
minutes or until just tender. Add mussels
and prawns and cook for 4-5 minutes
longer. Mix in 2 tablespoons fresh
coriander. Season to taste with black
pepper.

3   Cook fettuccine in boiling water in a
large saucepan following packet
directions. Drain, then spoon sauce over
fettuccine and sprinkle with remaining
fresh coriander. Serve immediately.

Serves 4

Accompany this simple, spicy
meal with a salad made of
your favourite vegetables.
You might like to try a salad
of raw spinach, orange
segments, thinly sliced
mushrooms and spring
onions, tossed in a light
vinaigrette dressing.

Spaghetti with Ratatouille Sauce,
Tuna Cannelloni, Seafood Fettuccine

PENNE, BACON AND BASIL

500 g/1 lb penne
1 tablespoon olive oil
2 cloves garlic, crushed
6 rashers bacon, chopped
2 tablespoons chopped fresh basil
60 g/2 oz chopped walnuts
freshly ground black pepper
30 g/1 oz grated Parmesan cheese

1   Cook penne in boiling water in a large saucepan following packet directions. Drain, set aside and keep warm.

2   Heat oil in a large frying pan and cook garlic over a medium heat for 1 minute. Add bacon and cook for 2-3 minutes longer or until bacon is crispy. Add basil, walnuts and penne to pan, season to taste with black pepper and toss to combine. Sprinkle with Parmesan cheese and serve immediately.

Penne, Bacon and Basil
Ravioli with Vegetable Medley

Serves 4

Ravioli with Vegetable Medley

500 g/1 lb ravioli of your choice
30 g/1 oz butter
2 cloves garlic, crushed
125 g/4 oz button mushrooms, halved
125 g/4 oz green beans, cut into
1 cm/^{1}/$_2$ in lengths
125 g/4 oz cherry tomatoes, quartered
freshly ground black pepper
30 g/1 oz grated Parmesan cheese

1   Cook ravioli in boiling water in a large saucepan following packet directions. Drain, set aside and keep warm.

2   Melt butter in a large frying pan and cook garlic and mushrooms for 2-3 minutes. Add beans and tomatoes, season to taste with black pepper and cook for 2 minutes longer.

3   Add ravioli and Parmesan cheese to pan and toss to combine. Serve immediately.

Serves 4

The microwave oven has made reheating pasta not only easy but successful in a way that it never was before. To reheat pasta in the microwave, place cooked pasta, with or without sauce, in a covered, microwave-safe dish and reheat on HIGH (100%), stirring once or twice, for 2-3 minutes, or until pasta is hot. The exact length of time will of course depend on how much pasta you are reheating.

Pork Pie

375 g/12 oz prepared shortcrust pastry
60 g/2 oz grated tasty cheese
(mature Cheddar)

PORK AND MUSHROOM FILLING
30 g/1 oz butter
1 onion, chopped
500 g/1 lb lean pork mince
1 cup/250 g/8 oz tomato purée
^{1}/$_2$ cup/125 mL/4 fl oz dry white wine
250 g/8 oz button mushrooms, sliced

MACARONI FILLING
185 g/6 oz macaroni
30 g/1 oz butter
2 tablespoons flour
1 cup/250 mL/8 fl oz hot milk
1 tablespoon chopped fresh parsley
freshly ground black pepper

1   Roll out pastry to fit a deep-sided 23 cm/9 in flan dish. Line pastry case with nonstick baking paper and weigh down with uncooked rice. Bake pastry case for 10-15 minutes, then remove rice and paper and set pastry case aside to cool.

2   To make Pork and Mushroom Filling, melt butter in a large saucepan and cook onion for 2-3 minutes, then add pork and cook, stirring to break up meat, for 10 minutes longer or until meat changes colour. Stir in tomato purée, wine and mushrooms. Bring meat mixture to simmering and simmer for 20 minutes.

3   To make Macaroni Filling, cook macaroni in boiling water in a large saucepan following packet directions. Drain and set aside. Melt butter in a saucepan over a medium heat, then stir in flour and cook for 1 minute. Stir in hot milk and cook, stirring constantly, for 4-5 minutes or until sauce thickens. Remove sauce from heat and stir in macaroni and parsley. Season to taste with black pepper.

4   Spread Pork and Mushroom Filling over base of pastry case, top with Macaroni Filling and sprinkle with cheese. Reduce oven temperature to 180°C/350°F/Gas 4 and bake pie for 25-30 minutes or until top is golden.

Serves 6

Oven temperature
200°C, 400°F, Gas 6

Pasta is a complex carbohydrate which means that it sustains and releases energy over a long period of time and so is a favoured food of athletes and others with high energy demands. Pasta itself is low in fat and calories; it's the sauce and other ingredients that you add that can do the damage. So, if you are watching the calories, choose sauces that are low in fat. Fresh vegetable sauces without cream and fresh tomato sauces are good choices. Remember to top pasta dishes with only a little cheese.

Below: Pork Pie
Below right: Red Pepper, Cheese and Fettuccine

Red Pepper, Cheese and Fettuccine

500 g/1 lb fettuccine
2 tablespoons oil
2 cloves garlic, crushed
2 red peppers, cut into strips
8 spring onions, cut into thin strips
1 teaspoon cracked black pepper
90 g/3 oz goat's cheese, crumbled

1   Cook fettuccine in boiling water in a large saucepan following packet directions. Drain, set aside and keep warm.

2   Heat oil in a large frying pan and cook garlic and red peppers for 2 minutes. Add spring onions and black pepper and cook for 1 minute longer. Add fettuccine and cheese to red pepper mixture and toss to combine. Serve immediately.

Serves 4

When buying goat's cheese, the colour of the cheese under the rind should be chalk-white. The cheese should be fresh and tangy, with no smell of ammonia.

Bean Lasagne

BEAN LASAGNE

Oven temperature
180°C, 350°F, Gas 4

12 spinach leaves, chopped
250 g/8 oz lasagne sheets
125 g/4 oz grated tasty cheese
(mature Cheddar)
2 tablespoons grated Parmesan cheese

TOMATO BEAN SAUCE
1 tablespoon olive oil
2 onions, chopped
2 cloves garlic, crushed
440 g/14 oz canned tomatoes, undrained
440 g/14 oz canned lima or butter beans,
drained and puréed
440 g/14 oz canned red kidney beans,
drained
1 teaspoon hot chilli sauce
1 teaspoon dried oregano

Serves 6

1   To make sauce, heat oil in a large frying pan and cook onions and garlic for 4-5 minutes or until onions are soft. Stir in tomatoes, lima, or butter, bean purée, red kidney beans, chilli sauce and oregano. Bring to the boil, then reduce heat and simmer, uncovered, for 10 minutes or until sauce reduces and thickens. Remove sauce from heat and set aside.

2   Place a little water in a saucepan and bring to the boil, add spinach and cook for 1-2 minutes or until spinach wilts. Drain and set aside. Cook lasagne sheets in boiling water in a large saucepan following packet directions. Drain.

3   Place one-third lasagne sheets in the base of a lightly greased, shallow ovenproof dish, then top with one-third of the bean sauce and half of the spinach. Repeat layers, then finish with a layer of lasagne sheets and remaining bean sauce. Sprinkle with tasty cheese (mature Cheddar) and Parmesan cheese. Bake for 30 minutes or until lasagne is heated through and top is golden.

QUICK FETTUCCINE WITH SCALLOPS

500 g/1 lb fettuccine
1 tablespoon finely chopped
fresh parsley

SCALLOP SAUCE
30 g/1 oz butter
1 red pepper, cut into strips
2 spring onions, finely chopped
1 cup/250 mL/8 fl oz cream (double)
500 g/1 lb scallops
freshly ground black pepper

1   Cook fettuccine in boiling water in a large saucepan following packet directions. Drain, set aside and keep warm.

2   To make sauce, melt butter in a large frying pan and cook red pepper and spring onions for 1-2 minutes. Add cream and bring to the boil, then reduce heat and simmer for 5 minutes or until sauce reduces slightly and thickens.

3   Stir scallops into sauce and cook for 2-3 minutes or until scallops are opaque. Season to taste with black pepper. Place fettuccine in a warm serving bowl, top with sauce and sprinkle with parsley.

Serves 4

A salad of mixed lettuces refreshes the palate and is the ideal accompaniment for this rich dish.

Quick Fettuccine with Scallops

SPAGHETTI WITH ASPARAGUS

500 g/1 lb wholemeal spaghetti
60 g/2 oz grated Parmesan cheese

ASPARAGUS SAUCE
1 tablespoon olive oil
1 clove garlic, crushed
440 g/14 oz canned tomatoes,
drained and chopped
315 g/10 oz canned
asparagus cuts (tips), drained
1 tablespoon chopped fresh parsley
1 tablespoon brown sugar
2 tablespoons red wine
freshly ground black pepper

1   Cook spaghetti in boiling water in a large saucepan following packet directions. Drain, set aside and keep warm.

2   To make sauce, heat oil in a frying pan and cook garlic over a medium heat for 1 minute. Stir in tomatoes, asparagus, parsley, sugar and wine. Bring to simmering, cover and simmer for 15-20 minutes or until sauce reduces and thickens. Season to taste with black pepper. Spoon sauce over spaghetti and top with Parmesan cheese. Serve immediately.

*Spaghetti with Asparagus,
Tuna Lasagne*

Serves 4

Tuna Lasagne

15 g/¹/₂ oz butter
2 stalks celery, finely chopped
1 onion, chopped
9 sheets instant (no precooking required) lasagne
440 g/14 oz canned tuna, drained and flaked
2 tablespoons grated tasty cheese (mature Cheddar)
1 teaspoon curry powder
¹/₂ teaspoon ground paprika

CURRY SAUCE
2 cups/500 mL/16 fl oz milk
1 cup/250 mL/8 fl oz water
30 g/1 oz butter
¹/₃ cup/45 g/1¹/₂ oz flour
2 teaspoons curry powder
2 eggs, beaten
2 tablespoons grated tasty cheese (mature Cheddar)
freshly ground black pepper

Serves 6

1   To make sauce, combine milk and water and set aside. Melt butter in a saucepan, stir in flour and curry powder and cook for 2-3 minutes. Remove pan from heat and whisk in milk mixture. Return sauce to heat and cook, stirring constantly, for 4-5 minutes or until sauce boils and thickens. Remove pan from heat and whisk in eggs and cheese. Season to taste with black pepper.

2   Melt butter in a frying pan and cook celery and onion for 4-5 minutes or until onion is soft. Spoon a little sauce over the base of a lightly greased shallow ovenproof dish. Top with three lasagne sheets and spread over half the tuna and half the celery mixture, then a layer of sauce. Repeat layers, finishing with a layer of lasagne, then sauce.

3   Combine cheese, curry powder and paprika, and sprinkle over lasagne. Bake for 30-35 minutes or until noodles are tender and top is golden.

Oven temperature
190°C, 375°F, Gas 5

This recipe freezes well. Thaw overnight in the refrigerator before reheating at 180°C, 350°F, Gas 4 for 30 minutes.

Pasta with Artichokes

375 g/12 oz spiral pasta
2 tablespoons Parmesan cheese

ARTICHOKE SAUCE
1 tablespoon olive oil
1 onion, chopped
2 cloves garlic, crushed
4 large ripe tomatoes, peeled and chopped
2 tablespoons chopped fresh basil
2 tablespoons chopped fresh parsley
440 g/14 oz canned artichoke hearts, drained and halved
freshly ground black pepper

Serves 4

1   To make sauce, heat oil in a saucepan and cook onion and garlic over a medium heat until onion is soft. Stir in tomatoes, basil and parsley and bring to the boil. Reduce heat, cover and simmer, stirring occasionally, for 30 minutes or until sauce reduces and thickens. Stir in artichokes and season to taste with black pepper.

2   Cook pasta in boiling water in a large saucepan following packet directions. Drain, spoon sauce over hot pasta, sprinkle with Parmesan cheese and serve immediately.

The globe artichoke is one of the most popular vegetables in Italy. It is actually a cultivated thistle grown for its edible, immature flower heads.
In this sauce the hard work has been taken out of preparing the artichokes by using canned ones.

MUSHROOM BOLOGNESE

500 g/1 lb spaghetti

BOLOGNESE SAUCE
2 tablespoons olive oil
220 g/7 oz mushrooms, sliced
1 carrot, finely chopped
1 onion, finely chopped
1 clove garlic, crushed
$^{1}/_{2}$ teaspoon chilli powder
500 g/1 lb lean beef mince
155 g/5 oz prosciutto or bacon,
finely chopped
ground nutmeg
$^{3}/_{4}$ cup/185 mL/6 fl oz dry red wine
$^{1}/_{2}$ cup/125 g/4 oz tomato paste (purée)
440 g/14 oz canned tomatoes,
undrained and mashed
$^{1}/_{2}$ cup/125 mL/4 fl oz water
freshly ground black pepper

You may wish to accompany this delicious main meal with freshly grated Parmesan cheese, a green salad and crusty bread.

1   To make sauce, heat oil in a large frying pan and cook mushrooms, carrot and onion for 4-5 minutes or until onion is soft. Stir in garlic and chilli powder and cook for 1 minute longer.

2   Add beef and prosciutto or bacon to pan and cook over a medium heat, stirring to break up meat, for 4-5 minutes or until meat changes colour. Drain off any fat and season to taste with nutmeg.

3   Stir wine, tomato paste (purée), tomatoes and water into pan. Bring to the boil, then reduce heat and simmer, stirring occasionally, for 30 minutes or until sauce reduces and thickens. Season to taste with black pepper.

4   Cook spaghetti in boiling water in a large saucepan following packet directions. Drain, place in warmed serving bowls, top with sauce and serve immediately.

Serves 6

Mushroom Bolognese

Spring Tagliatelle

Spring Tagliatelle

250 g/8 oz cauliflower florets
250 g/8 oz broccoli florets
250 g/8 oz tagliatelle
4 tablespoons olive oil
2 cloves garlic, crushed
1 small eggplant (aubergine),
cut into strips
$^1/_2$ red pepper, cut into strips
$^1/_2$ green pepper, cut into strips
2 tablespoons chopped fresh basil
freshly ground black pepper
30 g/1 oz grated fresh Parmesan cheese

1   Blanch cauliflower and broccoli in boiling water for 1 minute or cook in microwave for 1 minute. Drain and refresh under cold running water, drain again and set aside.

2   Cook tagliatelle in boiling water in a large saucepan following packet directions. Drain, set aside and keep warm.

3   Heat oil in a large frying pan and cook garlic and eggplant (aubergine), red pepper and green pepper over a medium heat for 4-5 minutes. Add tagliatelle, cauliflower, broccoli and basil to pan and toss to combine. Season to taste with black pepper and sprinkle with Parmesan cheese. Serve immediately.

Serves 4

This medley of lightly cooked vegetables, fresh basil and pasta makes a delectable combination. To complete the meal, serve with crusty bread and a salad of mixed lettuce and fresh herbs tossed in a garlicky dressing.

Cheesy Meatballs with Spaghetti

CHEESY MEATBALLS WITH SPAGHETTI

250 g/8 oz spaghetti

CHEESY MEATBALLS
500 g/1 lb lean beef mince
2 tablespoons finely chopped
fresh parsley
$^1/_2$ cup/60 g/2 oz grated Parmesan cheese
2 teaspoons tomato paste (purée)
1 egg, beaten

TOMATO SAUCE
15 g/$^1/_2$ oz butter
1 onion, finely chopped
2 teaspoons dried basil
1 teaspoon dried oregano
440 g/14 oz canned tomatoes,
undrained and mashed
2 tablespoons tomato paste (purée)
$^1/_2$ cup/125 mL/4 fl oz beef stock
$^1/_2$ cup/125 mL/4 fl oz white wine
1 teaspoon caster sugar
freshly ground black pepper

1   To make meatballs, place beef, parsley, Parmesan cheese, tomato paste (purée) and egg in a bowl, and mix to combine. Form mixture into small balls and cook in a nonstick frying pan for 4-5 minutes or until brown. Remove meatballs from pan and drain on absorbent kitchen paper.

2   To make sauce, melt butter in a large frying pan and cook onion, basil and oregano for 2-3 minutes or until onion is soft. Stir in tomatoes, tomato paste (purée), beef stock, wine and sugar. Bring to the boil, then reduce heat and simmer, stirring occasionally, for 30 minutes or until sauce reduces and thickens. Season to taste with black pepper. Add meatballs to sauce and cook for 5 minutes longer.

3   Cook spaghetti in boiling water in a large saucepan following packet directions. Drain, place in a warm serving bowl and top with meatballs and sauce. Serve immediately.

Serves 4

What's the easiest way to eat ribbon pasta? Firstly, serve it in a shallow bowl or on a plate with a slight rim. To ensure that the pasta stays hot while you are eating it, heat the plates before serving. To eat the pasta, slip a few strands on to your fork, then twirl them against the plate, or a spoon, into a ball – the trick is to take only small forkfuls and to wind the pasta tightly so that there are no dangling strands.

CHICKEN, PASTA TOSS

500 g/1 lb shell pasta
30 g/1 oz butter
1 onion, finely chopped
1 clove garlic, crushed
250 g/8 oz cooked chicken, shredded
$^1/_2$ cup/125 mL/4 fl oz chicken stock
6 spinach leaves, shredded
freshly ground black pepper
60 g/2 oz pine nuts, toasted

1   Cook pasta in boiling water in a large saucepan following packet directions. Drain, set aside and keep warm.

2   Melt butter in a large frying pan and cook onion and garlic, stirring, over a medium heat for 3-4 minutes. Add chicken and stock, and cook for 4-5 minutes longer.

3   Add spinach and pasta to pan, season to taste with black pepper and toss to combine. Sprinkle with pine nuts and serve immediately.

Serves 4

Chicken, Pasta Toss

This pretty pasta dish looks wonderful served with a salad of julienne carrots. To make the salad, cut 3 large carrots into strips and boil or microwave until just tender. Drain, refresh under cold running water, drain again and place in a salad bowl. Place 2 tablespoons lemon juice, 1 tablespoon Dijon mustard, 4 tablespoons olive oil and 1 tablespoon snipped fresh chives in a screwtop jar and shake to combine. Spoon over carrots and toss to combine. Cover and chill for 1 hour or until required.

BEEF LASAGNE

Oven temperature
190°C, 375°F, Gas 5

6 sheets instant (no precooking required)
lasagne
60 g/2 oz grated tasty cheese
(mature Cheddar)
2 tablespoons grated Parmesan cheese

MEAT SAUCE
2 teaspoons olive oil
1 onion, chopped
2 cloves garlic, crushed
2 rashers bacon, chopped
125 g/4 oz button mushrooms, sliced
500 g/1 lb lean beef mince
440 g/14 oz canned tomatoes,
undrained and mashed
$^1/_2$ cup/125 mL/4 fl oz red wine
$^1/_2$ teaspoon dried basil
$^1/_2$ teaspoon dried oregano
1 teaspoon sugar

SPINACH CHEESE SAUCE
30 g/1oz butter
2 tablespoons flour
1 cup/250 mL/8 fl oz milk
$^1/_2$ cup/125 mL/4 fl oz cream (single)
$^1/_2$ cup/60 g/2 oz grated tasty cheese
(mature Cheddar)
250 g/8 oz frozen spinach, thawed
and drained
freshly ground black pepper

As an accompaniment to
this substantial lasagne
choose something light, such
as a tomato and herb salad.

1   To make Meat Sauce, heat oil in a
large frying pan and cook, onion, garlic,
bacon and mushrooms over a medium
heat for 4-5 minutes or until onion is
soft.

2   Add beef to pan and cook, stirring to
break up meat, for 4-5 minutes or until
meat is brown. Combine tomatoes, wine,
basil, oregano and sugar, and pour into
pan with meat mixture. Bring to the boil,
then reduce heat, cover and simmer for
35 minutes or until sauce thickens.

3   To make Spinach Cheese Sauce,
melt butter in a saucepan and cook flour
for 1-2 minutes. Remove pan from heat
and stir in milk and cream. Cook,
stirring constantly, over a medium heat
for 4-5 minutes or until sauce boils and
thickens. Remove pan from heat and stir
in cheese and spinach. Season to taste
with black pepper.

4   To assemble lasagne, spread one-third
of the Spinach Cheese Sauce over base
of a lightly greased, shallow 28 x 18 cm/
11 x 7 in ovenproof dish. Top with three
lasagne sheets, spread half the Meat
Sauce over, then another third of the
Spinach Cheese Sauce. Top with
another three lasagne sheets and
remaining Meat Sauce. Place remaining
lasagne sheets over Meat Sauce and top
with remaining Spinach Cheese Sauce.

5   Combine tasty cheese (mature
Cheddar) and Parmesan cheese and
sprinkle over lasagne and bake for 40
minutes or until top is golden.

Serves 6

Right: Beef Lasagne

TORTELLINI WITH RED PEPPER SAUCE

500 g/1 lb tortellini

RED PEPPER SAUCE
1 tablespoon vegetable oil
1 onion, chopped
440 g/14 oz canned sweet red peppers,
drained and chopped
1 cup/250 mL/8 fl oz water
1 tablespoon honey
1 tablespoon chopped fresh oregano
freshly ground black pepper

1   Cook tortellini in boiling water in a large saucepan, following packet directions. Drain, set aside and keep warm.

2   To make sauce, heat oil in a small frying pan and cook onion, stirring, for 3 minutes or until onion is soft. Place red peppers, water, honey, oregano and onion in a food processor or blender and process to make a smooth sauce.

3   Pour pepper sauce into a large saucepan and heat over a medium heat for 4-5 minutes or until sauce is simmering. Season to taste with black pepper. Spoon sauce over tortellini and toss to combine.

Serves 4

Canned sweet red peppers are available from Continental delicatessens and some supermarkets. They are sometimes called pimentos.
You may wish to use fresh red peppers instead of the canned ones. You will require 4 large peppers for this recipe and they need to be roasted and the skin removed before making the sauce.

SAUCES

Nothing beats a bowl of perfectly cooked pasta topped with a delicious sauce and sprinkled with freshly grated Parmesan cheese. These sauces make pasta into something special and are sure to be popular.

Yogurt Herb Sauce

CREAMY PUMPKIN SAUCE

500 g/1 lb fettuccine

PUMPKIN SAUCE
250 g/8 oz pumpkin, cut into strips
2 cups/500 mL/16 fl oz cream (double)
125 g/4 oz pumpkin, cooked and mashed
$^1/_2$ teaspoon ground nutmeg
freshly ground black pepper
1 teaspoon snipped fresh chives

1   Cook fettuccine in boiling water in a large saucepan following packet directions. Drain, set aside and keep warm.

2   To make sauce, boil, steam or microwave pumpkin strips until just tender. Drain, refresh under cold running water and set aside.

3   Place cream in a large frying pan and bring to the boil. Reduce heat and simmer for 10-15 minutes or until cream is reduced by half. Whisk mashed pumpkin, nutmeg and black pepper to taste into cream and cook for 2-3 minutes longer. Then stir pumpkin strips and chives into sauce and cook for 2-3 minutes.

4   Spoon sauce over fettuccine and toss to combine. Serve immediately.

Serves 4

The people of Mantua in northern Italy have a reputation for being pumpkin eaters. This pretty pasta sauce would, no doubt, be much to their liking. Pumpkins, tomatoes, red and green peppers, beans and corn are all vegetables of the New World. They arrived in Italy during the sixteenth century.

YOGURT HERB SAUCE

500 g/1 lb mixed coloured spiral pasta

YOGURT HERB SAUCE
15 g/$^1/_2$ oz butter
1 small onion, chopped
1 clove garlic, crushed
2 tablespoons flour
$^1/_2$ cup/125 mL/4 fl oz vegetable stock
1 cup/200 g/6$^1/_2$ oz natural yogurt
2 tablespoons finely chopped
fresh parsley
2 tablespoons finely chopped fresh basil
2 tablespoons snipped fresh chives
freshly ground black pepper

1   Cook pasta in boiling water in a large saucepan following packet directions. Drain, set aside and keep warm.

2   To make sauce, melt butter in a saucepan and cook onion and garlic over a medium heat for 2-3 minutes. Stir in flour and stock and cook, stirring constantly, for 4-5 minutes longer or until sauce boils and thickens.

3   Remove pan from heat, stir in yogurt and cook over a low heat for 2-3 minutes longer. Mix in parsley, basil and chives and season to taste with black pepper. Spoon sauce over pasta and serve immediately.

Serves 4

This tasty low-kilojoule (calorie) sauce is also great spooned over steamed vegetables. If watching the kilojoules (calories) it makes an original alternative to white sauce. You may wish to use low-fat yogurt to further reduce fat and kilojoule (calorie) content.

CHICKEN LIVER SAUCE

30 g/1 oz butter
4 rashers bacon, chopped
1 onion, finely chopped
1 clove garlic, crushed
375 g/12 oz chicken livers, chopped
2 teaspoons flour
$^3/_4$ cup/185 mL/6 fl oz chicken stock
1 teaspoon tomato paste (purée)
1 teaspoon chopped fresh marjoram or
$^1/_2$ teaspoon dried marjoram
freshly ground black pepper
$^1/_4$ cup/60 g/2 oz sour cream

Serves 4

To serve, spoon sauce over pasta and garnish with fresh marjoram sprigs if desired. This sauce goes well with pastas such as rigatoni, penne and farfelle.

1 Melt butter in a saucepan and cook bacon, onion and garlic over a medium heat for 4-5 minutes or until onion is soft. Add chicken livers and cook, stirring, for 4-5 minutes or until livers change colour.

2 Stir in flour, then gradually blend in stock. Add tomato paste (purée), marjoram and black pepper to taste. Cover and cook, stirring occasionally, over a low heat for 10 minutes. Just prior to serving, stir in sour cream.

TOMATO SAUCE

1 tablespoon olive oil
1 onion, finely chopped
1 clove garlic, crushed
500 g/1 lb tomatoes, peeled and
roughly chopped
1 tablespoon tomato paste (purée)
$^1/_2$ teaspoon sugar
1 tablespoon chopped fresh basil
freshly ground black pepper

Serves 4

To serve, spoon sauce over pasta and toss to combine. Top with grated fresh Parmesan cheese and serve immediately. This sauce is delicious with any kind of pasta.

1 Heat oil in a saucepan and cook onion and garlic over a medium heat for 4-5 minutes or until onion is soft. Add tomatoes, tomato paste (purée), sugar and basil.

2 Bring sauce to simmering, cover and simmer, stirring occasionally, for 30 minutes or until sauce reduces and thickens. Season to taste with black pepper.

TOMATO BOLOGNESE SAUCE

2 tablespoons olive oil
2 rashers bacon, chopped
1 onion, chopped
1 carrot, chopped
1 stalk celery, chopped
1 clove garlic, crushed
250 g/8 oz lean beef mince
125 g/4 oz chicken livers, chopped
2 tablespoons tomato paste (purée)
$^1/_2$ cup/125 mL/4 fl oz dry white wine
$^1/_2$ cup/125 mL/4 fl oz beef or
chicken stock
pinch ground nutmeg
freshly ground black pepper

1 Heat oil in a large saucepan and cook bacon, stirring, over a medium heat for 3-4 minutes. Add onion, carrot, celery and garlic and cook, stirring, for 5 minutes longer or until vegetables start to brown.

2 Add beef mince to pan and cook, stirring to break up meat, for 5-6 minutes or until beef mince browns. Add chicken livers and cook for 2-3 minutes or until livers change colour.

3 Stir in tomato paste (purée), wine, stock and nutmeg. Bring sauce to simmering, cover and simmer for 30-40 minutes or until sauce reduces and thickens. Season to taste with black pepper.

Serves 4

To serve, spoon sauce over hot spaghetti and garnish with celery leaves if desired. This tomato-flavoured meat sauce is also excellent served with penne, macaroni, farfelle and rigatoni.

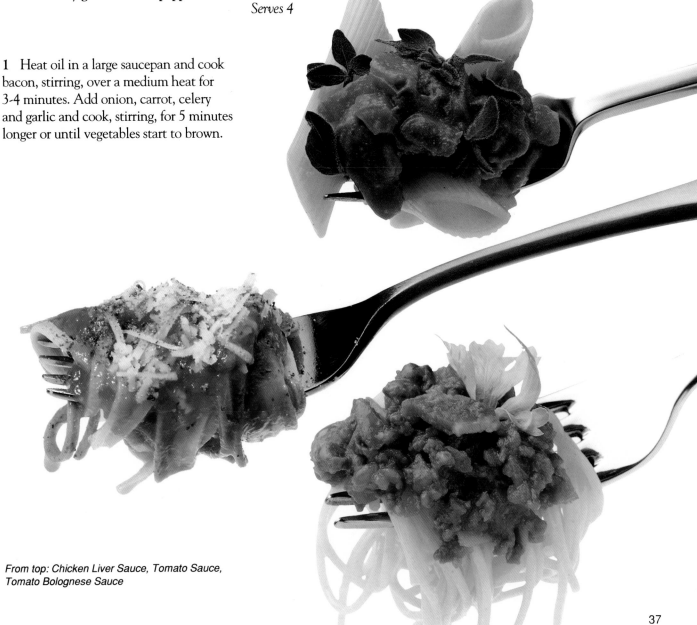

From top: Chicken Liver Sauce, Tomato Sauce, Tomato Bolognese Sauce

RAVIOLI WITH TUNA SAUCE

375 g/12 oz fresh or frozen
spinach ravioli
2 tablespoons grated Parmesan cheese

TUNA TOMATO SAUCE
1 teaspoon olive oil
1 onion, finely chopped
1 clove garlic, crushed
440 g/14 oz canned tomatoes,
undrained and mashed
1 tablespoon tomato paste (purée)
1 tablespoon dry red wine
1 teaspoon sugar
440 g/14 oz canned tuna, drained
and flaked
1 tablespoon finely chopped fresh parsley
1 tablespoon finely chopped fresh dill
freshly ground black pepper

1   Cook ravioli in boiling water in a large saucepan following packet directions. Drain, set aside and keep warm.

2   To make sauce, heat oil in a frying pan and cook onion and garlic over a medium heat for 4-5 minutes or until onion is soft. Stir in tomatoes, tomato paste (purée), wine and sugar. Bring to the boil, then add tuna, parsley and dill. Reduce heat and simmer for 10 minutes or until sauce reduces and thickens.

3   Place ravioli on a warmed serving platter, spoon sauce over, sprinkle with Parmesan cheese and serve immediately.

Serves 4

Don't keep this tuna sauce just for ravioli; try it spooned over penne, farfelle and conchigliette.

*Ravioli with Tuna Sauce,
Asparagus Sauce*

Asparagus Sauce

500 g/1 lb spaghetti
2 tablespoons grated Parmesan cheese

ASPARAGUS SAUCE
**500 g/1 lb fresh asparagus spears,
trimmed**
1 tablespoon olive oil
1 thick slice wholegrain bread, crumbed
**1 cup/250 mL/8 fl oz evaporated
skim milk**
60 g/2 oz grated mozzarella cheese
freshly ground black pepper

1   Cook spaghetti in boiling water in a large saucepan following packet directions. Drain, set aside and keep warm.

2   To make sauce, steam, boil or microwave asparagus until tender. Drain and refresh under cold running water. Cut asparagus into 2.5 cm/1 in pieces and set aside.

3   Heat oil in a frying pan and cook bread crumbs over a low heat, stirring constantly, for 2 minutes. Stir in milk and asparagus, and cook, stirring occasionally, over a medium heat for 5 minutes. Mix in cheese and season to taste with black pepper.

4   Place spaghetti on a warmed serving platter, spoon sauce over and toss gently to combine. Sprinkle with Parmesan cheese and serve immediately.

Serves 6

Nothing beats the taste of fresh asparagus. This is a wonderful way to use fresh asparagus in season while still retaining its delicate flavour.

Mushroom Pasta Sauce

375 g/12 oz fettuccine
2 tablespoons grated Parmesan cheese

MUSHROOM TOMATO SAUCE
60 g/2 oz butter
2 onions, chopped
**440 g/14 oz canned tomatoes, undrained
and mashed**
2 tablespoons tomato paste (purée)
125 g/4 oz mushrooms, sliced
4 zucchini (courgettes), sliced
**1 tablespoon chopped fresh oregano or
1 teaspoon dried oregano**
2 bay leaves
freshly ground black pepper

1   To make sauce, melt butter in a saucepan and cook onions for 3-4 minutes or until soft. Add tomatoes, tomato paste (purée), mushrooms, zucchini (courgettes), oregano and bay leaves and bring to the boil. Reduce heat, cover and simmer, stirring occasionally, for 30 minutes or until sauce reduces and thickens. Season to taste with black pepper.

2   Cook fettuccine in boiling water in a large saucepan following packet directions. Drain, then spoon sauce over fettuccine, sprinkle with Parmesan cheese and serve immediately.

Serves 4

Tomatoes, mushrooms, onions and zucchini (courgettes) combine to make a substantial vegetable sauce that is good with any type of pasta.

LIGHT MEALS

Pasta comes into its own as a fast food. These recipes take next to no time to prepare. In fact, many take less time to prepare and cook than many prepared convenience foods – and they taste wonderful.

Fettuccine with Green Sauce

375 g/12 oz fresh fettuccine

GREEN SAUCE
250 g/8 oz spinach, shredded
45 g/1¹/₂ oz butter
2 cloves garlic, crushed
1¹/₂ cups/375 mL/12 fl oz
cream (double)
125 g/4 oz grated fresh Parmesan cheese
freshly ground black pepper

1   Cook fettuccine in boiling water in a large saucepan following packet directions. Drain, set aside and keep warm.

2   To make sauce, boil, steam or microwave spinach for 2-3 minutes or until just cooked. Drain and set aside. Melt butter in a saucepan and cook garlic over a low heat for 2 minutes. Stir in cream and Parmesan cheese and cook, stirring constantly, for 2-3 minutes or until smooth. Stir spinach into sauce and season to taste with black pepper. Spoon sauce over fettuccine and toss to combine.

Serves 4

Fresh Parmesan cheese is available from continental delicatessens and some supermarkets. It is best purchased in a piece then grated as required. Once you have tried fresh Parmesan you will realise that it has a much milder and better flavour than the grated powder that comes in packets. If a recipe calls for fresh Parmesan cheese and it is unavailable, use about a third of the quantity of the packaged variety. If used in a sauce, you will notice it has a more grainy texture than fresh Parmesan.

Macaroni with Prosciutto

375 g/12 oz macaroni
45 g/1¹/₂ oz butter
2 cloves garlic, crushed
125 g/4 oz prosciutto or bacon,
cut into strips
6 sun-dried tomatoes, drained and
cut into strips
3 tablespoons chopped fresh basil
freshly ground black pepper

1   Cook macaroni in boiling water in a large saucepan following packet directions. Drain, set aside and keep warm.

2   Melt butter in a large saucepan and cook garlic and prosciutto or bacon over a medium heat for 5 minutes. Add tomatoes and basil and cook for 2 minutes longer.

3   Add prosciutto mixture to macaroni, season to taste with black pepper, and toss to combine. Serve immediately.

Serves 4

Prosciutto is an unsmoked, salted, air-cured ham. It is used in cooked dishes, or thinly sliced and served as part of an antipasto platter. It is also popular wrapped around melon and served as a starter.

*Fettuccine with Green Sauce,
Macaroni with Proscuitto*

ORIENTAL NOODLES AND VEGETABLES

500 g/1 lb Oriental noodles
1 tablespoon peanut oil
2 teaspoons grated fresh ginger
1 clove garlic, crushed
1 onion, sliced
1 carrot, sliced diagonally
2 stalks celery, sliced diagonally
90 g/3 oz bean sprouts
185 g/6 oz snow peas (mangetout),
trimmed
freshly ground black pepper

1   Cook noodles in boiling water in a large saucepan for 5-6 minutes or until cooked. Drain and set aside.

2   Heat oil in a wok or a large frying pan and stir-fry ginger and garlic for 1-2 minutes. Add onion and carrot and stir-fry for 4-5 minutes longer.

3   Toss in celery, bean sprouts and snow peas (mangetout) and cook for 2-3 minutes.

4   Stir in noodles and cook for 3-4 minutes or until noodles are heated. Season to taste with black pepper and serve immediately.

Serves 6

The flat Oriental noodles that have been used in this recipe are different from egg noodles; they are made from flour and water and are available from Chinese food stores.

TAGLIATELLE SALAD

250 g/8 oz fresh spinach tagliatelle
250 g/8 oz fresh plain tagliatelle
2 zucchini (courgettes),
cut into matchsticks
1 small red pepper, sliced
1 small green pepper, sliced
220 g/7 oz green beans, cooked

TOMATO AND BASIL DRESSING
4 ripe tomatoes, peeled and
roughly chopped
1 clove garlic, crushed
2 teaspoons olive oil
2 teaspoons red wine vinegar
2 tablespoons finely chopped fresh basil
1 tablespoon finely chopped fresh parsley
1 tablespoon snipped fresh chives
freshly ground black pepper

1   Cook both tagliatelles in boiling water in a large saucepan following packet directions. Rinse under cold running water, drain and set aside to cool completely.

2   Place cold tagliatelles, zucchini (courgettes), red and green peppers and beans in a large salad bowl.

3   To make dressing, place tomatoes, garlic, oil and vinegar in a food processor or blender and process until smooth. Stir in basil, parsley and chives and season to taste with black pepper. Spoon dressing over pasta and vegetables. Toss lightly to coat all ingredients with dressing.

Serves 6

As a luncheon, this salad tossed in a tomato and basil dressing needs only to be accompanied by crusty bread.

CREAMY MUSHROOMS AND PASTA

375 g/12 oz macaroni
3 tablespoons finely chopped
fresh parsley
2 tablespoons grated Parmesan cheese

CREAMY MUSHROOM SAUCE
2 teaspoons vegetable oil
1 onion, sliced
500 g/1 lb mushrooms, sliced
1 teaspoon paprika
2 tablespoons tomato paste (purée)
1 cup/250 mL/8 fl oz evaporated
skim milk
freshly ground black pepper

1   Cook macaroni in boiling water in a large saucepan following packet directions. Drain, set aside and keep warm.

2   To make sauce, heat oil in a large frying pan and cook onion and mushrooms for 5 minutes. Place paprika, tomato paste (purée) and milk in a bowl and whisk to combine. Stir into mushroom mixture and cook, stirring, over a low heat for 5 minutes. Season to taste with black pepper.

3   Place pasta in a heated serving dish and spoon sauce over. Toss to combine and sprinkle with parsley and Parmesan cheese. Serve immediately.

Serves 4

Creamy mushroom sauce and hot pasta – food that dreams are made of! And the best thing about this recipe is that it uses evaporated milk to make it creamy and so is lower in fat and cholesterol.
A green salad and crusty bread will complete your meal.

Oriental Noodles and Vegetables, Tagliatelle Salad, Creamy Mushrooms and Pasta

PEPPERONI TOSS

375 g/12 oz spaghetti
1 tablespoon olive oil
1 onion, finely chopped
90 g/3 oz black olives, chopped
125 g/4 oz pepperoni salami, chopped

1   Cook spaghetti in boiling water in a large saucepan following packet directions. Drain, set aside and keep warm.

2   Heat oil in a large frying pan and cook onion over a medium heat for 5-6 minutes or until onion is transparent. Add olives and salami and cook for 2 minutes longer.

3   Add spaghetti to pan and toss to combine. Serve immediately.

It is believed that salami originated in the Grecian town of Salamis. Pepperoni, one of the most used salamis, is made from ground pork and beef and flavoured with ground red pepper. Its popularity is due to the fact that it is the salami most often used on pizza.

Pepperoni Toss

Serves 4

Tortellini with Parsley Butter

TORTELLINI WITH PARSLEY BUTTER

500 g/1 lb tortellini
2 tablespoons olive oil
125 g/4 oz grated fresh Parmesan cheese
125 g/4 oz butter, cut into small cubes
pinch nutmeg
30 g/1 oz fresh parsley, chopped
freshly ground black pepper

1   Place tortellini and olive oil in a large saucepan of boiling water and cook following packet directions. Drain and place in a large serving bowl.

2   Top tortellini with Parmesan cheese, butter, nutmeg, parsley and black pepper to taste. Toss to combine and serve immediately.

Serves 4

There is a legend that says tortellini was created to honour Venus' bellybutton. Apparently, a Bolognan innkeeper was so inflamed with this beautiful young woman that after showing her to her room he then spied on her through the keyhole as she was undressing; but all he could see was her bellybutton. He rushed to his kitchen and created tortellini as a memento to Venus' beauty.

Pasta Shells with Anchovy Sauce,
Macaroni with Tomato Sauce

PASTA SHELLS WITH ANCHOVY SAUCE

500 g/1 lb small shell pasta
60 g/2 oz grated fresh Parmesan cheese

ANCHOVY SAUCE
2 tablespoons olive oil
3 onions, chopped
1 clove garlic, crushed
¹/₂ cup/125 mL/4 fl oz dry white wine
8 canned anchovies
1 tablespoon chopped fresh rosemary
leaves or 1 teaspoon dried rosemary
1 cup/250 mL/8 fl oz beef or
chicken stock
1 fresh red chilli, seeded and
cut into rings

1   Cook pasta shells in boiling water in a large saucepan following packet directions. Drain, set aside and keep warm.

2   To make sauce, heat oil in a large frying pan and cook onions and garlic over a medium heat for 10 minutes or until onions are soft. Stir in wine and anchovies and bring to the boil. Boil for 2-3 minutes or until wine reduces by half.

3   Stir in rosemary and stock and bring back to the boil. Boil until sauces reduces and thickens slightly. Add chilli and pasta to sauce, toss to combine, sprinkle with Parmesan cheese and serve immediately.

Serves 4

Anchovies come preserved in oil or salt. Once opened, canned anchovies can be kept, covered with olive oil, in the refrigerator. Anchovies preserved in salt should be rinsed well before using.
In Italy and France fresh anchovies are popular.

MACARONI WITH TOMATO SAUCE

500 g/1 lb wholemeal macaroni

CHUNKY TOMATO SAUCE
2 tablespoons olive oil
1 onion, chopped
1 clove garlic, crushed
2 x 440 g/14 oz canned Italian-style
tomatoes, undrained and mashed
¹/₄ cup/60 mL/2 fl oz dry white wine
1 tablespoon chopped fresh basil
freshly ground black pepper

1   Cook macaroni in boiling water in a large saucepan following packet directions. Drain, set aside and keep warm.

2   To make sauce, heat oil in a frying pan and cook onion for 3-4 minutes or until soft. Stir in garlic, tomatoes and wine and cook, stirring constantly, over a medium heat for 5 minutes. Bring to the boil, then reduce heat and simmer, uncovered, for 10-15 minutes or until sauce reduces and thickens. Add basil and season to taste with black pepper.

3   Add sauce to hot macaroni and toss to combine. Serve immediately.

Serves 4

This fresh-tasting tomato sauce is delicious with any dried pasta. You might like to try serving it with bucatini, the Italian macaroni that is long like spaghetti, but thicker and hollow.

RED PEPPER FRITTATA

Oven temperature
180°C, 350°F, Gas 4

220 g/7 oz fettuccine
1 1/2 cups/375 mL/12 fl oz milk
1/2 cup/125 mL/4 fl oz cream (double)
6 eggs, lightly beaten
2 tablespoons finely chopped
fresh parsley
1 red pepper, chopped
freshly ground black pepper

1   Cook fettuccine in boiling water in a large saucepan following packet directions. Drain and set aside.

2   Place milk, cream and eggs in a bowl and whisk to combine. Stir in parsley, red pepper, fettuccine and black pepper to taste.

3   Pour frittata mixture into a greased 23 cm/9 in flan dish and bake for 25-30 minutes or until frittata is set.

Red Pepper Frittata

Serves 4

Rigatoni with Pumpkin

RIGATONI WITH PUMPKIN

500 g/1 lb rigatoni
90 g/3 oz butter
250 g/8 oz pumpkin, cut into
small cubes
1 tablespoon snipped fresh chives
pinch ground nutmeg
30 g/1 oz grated fresh Parmesan cheese
freshly ground black pepper

1   Cook rigatoni in boiling water in a large saucepan following packet directions. Drain, set aside and keep warm.

2   Melt 60 g/2 oz butter in a large saucepan and cook pumpkin over a medium heat for 5-10 minutes or until tender.

3   Stir chives, nutmeg, Parmesan cheese, black pepper to taste, rigatoni and remaining butter into pumpkin mixture and toss to combine. Serve immediately.

Serves 4

You might like to make this pasta dish using carrots instead of pumpkin. The taste will be different, but just as delicious.

HAM AND CHEESE PIE

Oven temperature
180°C, 350°F, Gas 4

Another good way to use leftover pasta. This delicious pie is perfect for a winter's lunch or Sunday night tea around the fireside. Served with crusty bread and a salad of mixed lettuces and herbs, it is sure to be popular.

250 g/8 oz macaroni
3 eggs
125 g/4 oz grated tasty cheese
(mature Cheddar)
2 cups/500 mL/16 fl oz milk
$^1/_2$ cup/125 mL/4 fl oz cream
125 g/4 oz ham, chopped
1 tablespoon snipped fresh chives
freshly ground black pepper
30 g/1 oz butter

1   Cook macaroni in boiling water in a large saucepan following packet directions. Drain and place in a greased ovenproof baking dish.

2   Place eggs, cheese, milk, cream, ham, chives and black pepper to taste in a bowl and mix to combine. Pour over macaroni and dot top of pie with butter. Bake for 40 minutes or until pie is set.

Serves 4

NUTTY VERMICELLI WITH BROCCOLI

500 g/1 lb vermicelli noodles
250 g/8 oz broccoli, broken into florets
30 g/1 oz butter
4 spring onions, finely chopped
2 cloves garlic, crushed
1 teaspoon chilli paste (sambal oelek)
60 g/2 oz blanched almonds, chopped
$^1/_4$ cup/60 mL/2 fl oz white wine
freshly ground black pepper

1   Cook vermicelli in boiling water in a large saucepan following packet directions. Drain, set aside and keep warm.

2   Boil, steam or microwave broccoli until just tender. Drain and refresh under cold running water. Drain again and set aside. Melt butter in a large frying pan and cook spring onions, garlic, chilli paste (sambal oelek) and almonds, stirring, over a medium heat for 2 minutes. Stir in wine and cook for 3 minutes longer. Add broccoli and vermicelli, toss to combine and cook for 3-4 minutes. Season to taste with black pepper.

Serves 4

The crunch of almonds, the fresh taste of broccoli and a touch of chilli make a superb combination when teamed with vermicelli in this quick and easy, light meal.

Tortellini and Avocado Cream

TORTELLINI AND AVOCADO CREAM

500 g/1 lb tortellini

AVOCADO CREAM
1/2 ripe avocado, stoned and peeled
1/4 cup/60 mL/2 fl oz cream (double)
30 g/1 oz grated fresh Parmesan cheese
1 teaspoon lemon juice
freshly ground black pepper

1   Cook tortellini in boiling water in a large saucepan following packet directions. Drain, set aside and keep warm.

2   To make Avocado Cream, place avocado, cream, Parmesan cheese and lemon juice in a food processor or blender and process until smooth. Season to taste with black pepper.

3   Place tortellini in a warm serving bowl, add Avocado Cream and toss to combine. Serve immediately.

Serves 4

Avocado puréed with cream and Parmesan cheese makes a smooth rich sauce that is sure to be a hit with all avocado lovers. It is best to make this sauce just prior to serving, so that it does not discolour.

Spaghetti Carbonara

Spaghetti Carbonara

185 g/6 oz slices ham, cut into strips
4 eggs
$^1/_3$ cup/90 mL/3 fl oz cream (single)
90 g/3 oz grated fresh Parmesan cheese
500 g/1 lb spaghetti
freshly ground black pepper

There are several stories concerning the origins of this classic dish. The most romantic of these is that it was a dish created by the 'carbonari' – or charcoal makers – of Italy. The story goes that, as the dish requires little cooking and all the ingredients are transportable, the carbonari were able to cook it over an open fire.

1   Cook ham in a nonstick frying pan for 2-3 minutes. Place eggs, cream and Parmesan cheese in a bowl and beat lightly to combine.

2   Cook spaghetti in boiling water in a large saucepan following packet directions. Drain spaghetti, add egg mixture and ham and toss so that the heat of the spaghetti cooks the sauce. Season to taste with black pepper and serve immediately.

Serves 4

Macaroni with Basil

MACARONI WITH BASIL

375 g/12 oz wholemeal macaroni
1 tablespoon olive oil
2 cloves garlic, crushed
250 g/8 oz button mushrooms, sliced
6 sun-dried tomatoes, drained and
cut into strips
2 tablespoons chopped fresh basil
freshly ground black pepper

1   Cook macaroni in boiling water in a large saucepan following packet directions. Drain, set aside and keep warm.

2   Heat oil in a large frying pan and cook garlic, mushrooms and tomatoes over a medium heat for 4-5 minutes. Stir in basil and season to taste with black pepper.

3   Add macaroni to mushroom mixture and toss to combine. Serve immediately.

Serves 4

Basil originally came from India, where it is still regarded as a sacred herb. It was known in ancient times in southern Europe, and in Italy it symbolised love. Traditionally, a girl would place a pot in her window as an invitation to her lover to call on her.

TUNA-FILLED SHELLS

16 giant pasta shells

TUNA FILLING
250 g/8 oz ricotta cheese, drained
440 g/14 oz canned tuna in brine,
drained and flaked
$1/2$ red pepper, diced
1 tablespoon chopped capers
1 teaspoon snipped fresh chives
4 tablespoons grated Swiss cheese
pinch ground nutmeg
freshly ground black pepper
2 tablespoons grated fresh
Parmesan cheese

1   Cook 8 pasta shells in a large saucepan of boiling water until al dente. Drain, rinse under cold running water and drain again. Set aside, not overlapping. Repeat with remaining shells.

2   To make filling, place ricotta cheese and tuna in a bowl and mix to combine. Mix in red pepper, capers, chives and 2 tablespoons grated Swiss cheese, nutmeg and black pepper to taste.

3   Fill each shell with ricotta mixture, and place in a lightly greased, shallow ovenproof dish. Sprinkle with Parmesan cheese and remaining Swiss cheese. Place under a preheated grill and cook until cheese melts.

Makes 16 filled shells

These filled shells are fun to eat hot or cold as finger food, or they can be served with a sauce as a first course.

Tuna-filled Shells

54

Spirelli with Ham

SPIRELLI WITH HAM

500 g/1 lb fresh or 410 g/13 oz
dried spirelli or spiral pasta
2 teaspoons olive oil
315 g/10 oz ham, cut into strips
6 canned artichoke hearts,
sliced lengthwise
3 eggs, beaten with 1 tablespoon grated
fresh Parmesan cheese
freshly ground black pepper

1   Cook spirelli in boiling water in a large saucepan following packet directions. Drain, set aside and keep warm.

2   Heat oil in a frying pan and cook ham and artichokes for 1-2 minutes.

3   Add spirelli to pan and toss to combine. Remove from heat and quickly stir in egg mixture. Season to taste with black pepper. Serve as soon as the eggs start to stick to spirelli – this will take only a few seconds.

Serves 4

It is said that the four-pronged fork was invented by Ferdinand II, the King of Naples, so that spaghetti could be eaten in a more refined and elegant fashion.

SALADS

Pasta salads make wonderful starters and main courses, and are hard to beat as an accompaniment. Served either at room temperature or chilled, they look and taste marvellous as picnic fare or for a buffet.

Warm Pasta and Salami Salad

WARM PASTA AND SALAMI SALAD

250 g/8 oz large shell pasta
1 tablespoon olive oil
2 cloves garlic, crushed
60 g/2 oz pine nuts
125 g/4 oz salami, thinly sliced
1 tablespoon chopped fresh parsley

1 Cook pasta in boiling water in a large saucepan following packet directions. Drain, set aside and keep warm.

2 Heat oil in a large frying pan and cook garlic and pine nuts, stirring constantly, over a medium heat for 1-2 minutes. Remove pan from heat and stir in salami and parsley. Add salami mixture to pasta and toss to combine. Serve warm.

Serves 4 as a light meal

Warm salads are perfect for winter days when only a light meal is required. This one is great accompanied by a salad of lettuce, olives and tomatoes.

SEAFOOD AND DILL SALAD

750 g/1 lb firm white fish fillets,
cut into 2.5 cm/1 in cubes
2 tablespoons lemon juice
2 tablespoons finely chopped fresh dill
pinch cayenne pepper
freshly ground black pepper
125 g/4 oz spinach fettuccine
125 g/4 oz tomato fettuccine
125 g/4 oz plain fettuccine
3 zucchini (courgettes), cut into matchsticks
2 carrots, cut into matchsticks
2 stalks celery, cut into matchsticks

DILL DRESSING
1 teaspoon Dijon mustard
2 tablespoons finely chopped fresh dill
2 tablespoons lemon juice
4 tablespoons vegetable oil
freshly ground black pepper

1 Place fish, lemon juice, dill, cayenne pepper and black pepper to taste in a bowl. Toss to combine and set aside to marinate for 40 minutes.

2 Cook spinach, tomato and plain fettuccine together in boiling water in a large saucepan following packet directions. Drain, rinse under cold running water, then drain again and set aside to cool completely.

3 Steam or microwave zucchini (courgettes), carrots and celery separately for 2-3 minutes or until just tender. Refresh under cold running water and set aside to cool completely.

4 Drain fish and place fish, fettuccine, zucchini (courgettes), carrots and celery in a large salad bowl.

5 To make dressing, place mustard, dill, lemon juice, oil and black pepper to taste in a screwtop jar and shake to combine. Pour dressing over salad and toss gently. Serve immediately.

Serves 6 as a main meal

A salad of pasta and fish is a meal in itself. It makes a wonderful lunch or supper dish when served with warm crusty bread, a green salad and a glass of chilled white wine.

Multi-coloured Pasta Salad

90 g/3 oz plain shell pasta
90 g/3 oz spinach shell pasta
90 g/3 oz tomato shell pasta
6 spring onions, chopped
1 small red pepper, diced
1 small green pepper, diced

FRENCH DRESSING
2 tablespoons olive oil
4 tablespoons lemon juice
4 tablespoons white wine vinegar
$^1/_4$ teaspoon dry mustard powder
$^1/_2$ teaspoon sugar
freshly ground black pepper

1   Cook plain, spinach and tomato pasta together in boiling water in a large saucepan following packet directions. Drain, rinse under cold running water, then drain again and set aside to cool completely.

2   To make dressing, place oil, lemon juice, vinegar, mustard, sugar and black pepper to taste in a screwtop jar and shake to combine.

3   Place pasta shells, spring onions and red and green pepper in a salad bowl. Pour dressing over and toss to combine.

Serves 6 as an accompaniment

To prevent pasta that is to be used in a salad from sticking together, rinse it under cold running water immediately after draining.

Chicken Grape Salad

250 g/8 oz small shell pasta
1.5 kg/3 lb chicken, cooked and cooled
250 g/8 oz seedless green grapes
1 tablespoon chopped fresh tarragon
3 tablespoons mayonnaise
3 tablespoons natural yogurt
freshly ground black pepper

1   Cook pasta in boiling water in a large saucepan following packet directions. Drain, rinse under cold running water, then drain again and set aside to cool completely.

2   Remove skin from chicken and discard. Strip flesh from chicken and chop. Place pasta, chicken, grapes and tarragon in a bowl and toss to combine.

3   Place mayonnaise, yogurt and black pepper to taste in a small bowl and mix to combine. Spoon over chicken mixture and toss to coat all ingredients. Serve at room temperature.

Serves 6 as a main meal

Moist chunks of chicken, green grapes and tarragon tossed in a light dressing combine the flavours of summer in this scrumptious salad.

Avocado Salmon Salad

375 g/12 oz bow pasta
1 large avocado, stoned, peeled
and roughly chopped
1 teaspoon finely grated orange rind
2 tablespoons fresh orange juice
freshly ground black pepper
4 slices smoked salmon
4 sprigs fresh dill
1 orange, segmented

1   Cook pasta in boiling water in a large saucepan following packet directions. Drain, rinse under cold running water, then drain again and set aside to cool completely.

2   Place avocado, orange rind, orange juice and black pepper to taste in a food processor or blender and process until smooth.

3   Place pasta in a bowl, top with avocado mixture and toss to combine. Roll salmon slices into cornets and fill with a dill sprig. Divide salad between four serving plates and top with salmon cornets and orange segments.

Serves 4 as a light meal

Chicken Grape Salad,
Avocado Salmon Salad

CHILLI BROAD BEAN SALAD

375 g/12 oz small shell pasta
1 tablespoon vegetable oil
250 g/8 oz shelled or frozen broad beans
1 teaspoon chilli paste (sambal selek)
1¹/₂ cups/375 mL/12 fl oz chicken stock
6 radishes, thinly sliced
2 tablespoons chopped fresh parsley
30 g/1 oz grated fresh Parmesan cheese

GARLIC DRESSING
¹/₄ cup/60 mL/2 fl oz olive oil
1 tablespoon cider vinegar
1 clove garlic, crushed
freshly ground black pepper

1   Cook pasta in boiling water in a large saucepan following packet directions. Drain, rinse under cold running water, then drain again and set aside to cool completely.

2   Heat oil in a large frying pan and cook broad beans and chilli paste over a medium heat for 3 minutes. Stir in stock, bring to simmering, cover and simmer for 10 minutes. Drain off any remaining liquid and set aside to cool.

3   To make dressing, place oil, vinegar, garlic and black pepper to taste in a screwtop jar. Shake well to combine.

4   Place pasta, broad bean mixture, radishes, parsley and Parmesan cheese in a salad bowl. Pour dressing over and toss to combine.

Served with a tomato salad and garlic bread, this salad of pasta and beans with a hint of chilli makes a substantial main meal.

Serves 4 as a main meal

TUNA ANCHOVY SALAD

250 g/8 oz wholemeal pasta spirals
6 canned anchovies, drained
12 black olives
220 g/7 oz canned tuna, drained
1 tablespoon chopped fresh parsley
1 tablespoon snipped fresh chives
1 hard-boiled egg, cut in wedges

MUSTARD DRESSING
1 teaspoon Dijon mustard
1 clove garlic, crushed
1 tablespoon white wine vinegar
1/4 cup/60 mL/2 fl oz olive oil
freshly ground black pepper

1   Cook pasta in boiling water in a large saucepan following packet directions. Drain, rinse under cold running water, then drain again and set aside to cool completely.

2   Cut anchovies in half lengthwise. Wrap an anchovy strip around each olive. Place pasta, anchovy-wrapped olives, tuna, parsley and chives in a salad bowl.

3   To make dressing, place mustard, garlic, vinegar, oil and black pepper to taste in a screwtop jar and shake well. Pour dressing over salad and toss to combine. Top with egg wedges.

Serves 4 as a light meal

Made from store cupboard ingredients, this variation on a 'salade niçoise' brings together the tastes of the Mediterranean. Serve with herbed bread and a salad of mixed lettuces for an easy and stylish lunch.

CHICKEN PASTA SALAD

155 g/5 oz plain tagliatelle
155 g/5 oz spinach tagliatelle
155 g/5 oz tomato tagliatelle
2 tablespoons olive oil
2 red onions, cut into eighths
2 cloves garlic, crushed
500 g/1 lb chicken breast fillets, chopped
1 tablespoon finely chopped fresh
oregano or 1 teaspoon dried oregano
1 tablespoon finely chopped fresh basil
or 1 teaspoon dried basil
440 g/14 oz canned artichoke hearts,
drained and halved
1 red pepper, cut into strips
90 g/3 oz green olives, drained
freshly ground black pepper

Serves 6 as a main meal

Make this colourful salad of mixed pasta, vegetables and chicken in summer when fresh basil and oregano are at their best. As a final touch, top with grated fresh Parmesan cheese.

1   Cook plain, spinach and tomato tagliatelle together in boiling water in a large saucepan following packet directions. Drain, rinse under cold running water, then drain again and set aside to cool completely.

2   Heat oil in a large frying pan and cook onions and garlic, stirring, over a medium heat for 2-3 minutes. Add chicken, oregano and basil and cook, stirring, for 10 minutes longer or until chicken is cooked. Remove pan from heat and set aside to cool completely. Place cooked chicken mixture, artichokes, red pepper, olives and tagliatelle in a large salad bowl. Season to taste with black pepper and toss to combine.

VEGETABLE PASTA SALAD

500 g/1 lb small pasta shapes
of your choice
250 g/8 oz broccoli, broken into florets
250 g/8 oz cherry tomatoes, halved
6 spring onions, cut into
2.5 cm/1 in lengths
12 black olives

RED WINE DRESSING
2 tablespoons red wine vinegar
1/4 cup/125 mL/4 fl oz olive oil
2 tablespoons grated fresh
Parmesan cheese
1 clove garlic, crushed
freshly ground black pepper

Serves 8 as an accompaniment

A delicious salad that is equally good as a light vegetarian meal for four. For a garden lunch, accompany with crusty wholemeal rolls and finish with fresh fruit.

1   Cook pasta in boiling water in a large saucepan following packet directions. Drain, rinse under cold running water, then drain again and set aside to cool completely.

2   Boil, steam or microwave broccoli for 2-3 minutes or until it just changes colour. Refresh under cold running water. Drain, then dry on absorbent kitchen paper.

3   To make dressing, place vinegar, oil, Parmesan cheese, garlic and black pepper to taste in a screwtop jar and shake to combine.

4   Place pasta, broccoli, tomatoes, spring onions and olives in a salad bowl. Pour dressing over and toss to combine.

Chicken Pasta Salad,
Vegetable Pasta Salad

DESSERTS

*Pasta for dessert? These two dishes make the most of
pasta and provide economic and imaginative desserts – just
the thing to fill hungry teenagers.*

Apple Lasagne

Apricot Orange
Pudding

Apple Lasagne

64

APPLE LASAGNE

750 g/1¹/₂ lb green apples
30 g/1 oz butter
60 g/2 oz butter
¹/₄ teaspoon ground nutmeg
6 sheets lasagne
30 g/1 oz walnuts, finely chopped
2 tablespoons icing sugar, sifted

EGG CUSTARD
1¹/₄ cups/315 mL/10 fl oz milk
1 egg
1 egg yolk
1 tablespoon cornflour
1 tablespoon caster sugar

1 Cook lasagne in boiling water in a large saucepan following packet directions. Drain and set aside.

2 To make custard, heat milk in a saucepan and bring to simmering. Place egg, egg yolk, cornflour and sugar in a bowl and whisk to combine. Whisk hot milk into egg mixture. Return custard to saucepan and cook, stirring constantly, over a low heat for 4-5 minutes or until custard thickens. Remove saucepan from heat.

3 Spread 2 tablespoons custard over base of a shallow ovenproof dish, then layer lasagne sheets and apples into dish, finishing with a layer of apple. Pour remaining custard over lasagne and sprinkle with walnuts. Bake for 25 minutes. Serve hot or warm, sprinkled with icing sugar.

Serves 4

Oven temperature
190°C, 375°F, Gas 5

Layers of apples, lasagne and custard combine to make this filling and satisfying dessert.

APRICOT ORANGE PUDDING

125 g/4 oz dried apricots
1 cup/250 mL/8 fl oz warm water
cinnamon stick
2 tablespoons fresh orange juice
2 teaspoons finely grated orange rind
¹/₂ cup/90 g/3 oz soft brown sugar
2 teaspoons arrowroot blended with
2 teaspoons water
30 g/1 oz bread crumbs, made
from stale bread
125 g/4 oz tagliatelle
60 g/2 oz walnuts, ground
30 g/1 oz butter, melted

1 Place apricots in a bowl, pour warm water over and set aside to soak for 1 hour. Drain apricots and reserve liquid. Place apricots, 2 tablespoons reserved liquid, cinnamon stick, orange juice, orange rind and 1 tablespoon brown sugar

in a saucepan. Bring to the boil, then reduce heat, cover and simmer for 10-15 minutes or until apricots are tender.

2 Stir arrowroot mixture into apricot mixture and cook for 2-3 minutes longer or until mixture thickens. Remove pan from heat and set aside to cool.

3 Cook tagliatelle in boiling water in a large saucepan following packet directions. Drain and set aside.

4 Coat a buttered 20 cm/8 in soufflé dish with bread crumbs. Place one-third tagliatelle in base of soufflé dish and top with half apricot mixture. Repeat layers, sprinkle with walnuts and remaining sugar, and top with remaining tagliatelle. Pour butter over pudding and bake for 25 minutes. Turn onto a plate and cut into wedges to serve.

Oven temperature
190°C, 375°F, Gas 5

Serves 6

HOMEMADE PASTA

1   Place eggs in a large bowl and whisk to combine. Sift flour and salt into egg mixture.

4 large eggs
410 g/13 oz flour
large pinch salt
water

2   Using a fork first and then your hands, incorporate eggs into flour to form a coarse dough.

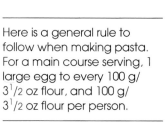

Here is a general rule to follow when making pasta. For a main course serving, 1 large egg to every 100 g/ 3^1/2 oz flour, and 100 g/ 3^1/2 oz flour per person.

3   Turn dough onto a lightly floured surface and knead by hand for 6-8 minutes or until a smooth elastic dough is formed. The dough can also be kneaded in the food processor for 2-3 minutes. Cover dough with a cloth and set aside to rest at room temperature for 15 minutes. Divide dough into manageable pieces and roll out either by hand or using a pasta machine, then use as required.

Serves 4

'Pasta is cooked when it is "al dente", that is tender but with resistance to the bite.'

FLAVOURED PASTA

TOMATO PASTA

Beat $2^1/_2$ tablespoons concentrated tomato paste into eggs, then follow method as for making Homemade Pasta.

SPINACH PASTA

Cook 75 g/$2^1/_2$ oz spinach, then drain thoroughly and squeeze to remove as much moisture as possible. Purée spinach with a pinch of nutmeg, then combine with eggs and follow method as for making Homemade Pasta.

WHOLEMEAL PASTA

Use half white flour and half wholemeal flour. Follow method as for making Homemade Pasta.

To make Herb Pasta, add 3 teaspoons of chopped fresh herbs to the eggs. Use either a single herb, such as parsley, or mixed herbs.

'Homemade pasta does not dry successfully, as the high moisture content makes the pasta dry out too quickly and crack.'

ROLLING PASTA

As well as experiencing the pleasure of making it yourself, an advantage of homemade pasta is the ranges of shapes you can create. You can roll pasta either by hand or using a pasta machine.

ROLLING BY HAND

If you are going to roll pasta by hand you will need a long rolling pin and a large work surface. Lightly flour the work surface then, using your hands, press the dough flat and roll it out, maintaining a circular shape. Keep rolling until the dough is a large thin sheet that is almost transparent – it should be thin enough to be able to read a newspaper through it! As you roll the dough, let some of it hang over the edge of the work surface – this helps to stretch it.

USING A PASTA MACHINE

1 Make the dough as for Homemade Pasta and divide dough into manageable pieces. As a general rule, divide the dough into as many pieces as the number of eggs used to make the dough. Set the rollers of the pasta machine on the widest setting and feed the dough through. Fold the rolled dough into quarters to make a square.

2 Feed the dough through the machine again, then fold again. Repeat folding and rolling of dough 4-5 times or until you have a shiny, smooth and elastic dough. Close the rollers a notch at a time and roll the dough thinner and thinner until the desired thickness is reached. Set aside to dry for 10-15 minutes.

3 To cut, using a pasta machine, feed each strip of pasta through the appropriate blades. As the strips of dough emerge from the machine catch them on your hand.

If making lasagne or filled pasta, use the pasta immediately. Otherwise, place on a clean cloth and set aside to dry at room temperature for 30 minutes or until dough is dry enough to prevent sticking, but is not brittle.

'To roll pasta by hand you need a long rolling pin and a large work surface.'

Cooking Pasta

*The secret to cooking pasta is to use lots of water and a large
saucepan so the pasta does not stick together.*

Leftover pasta and sauces
can be mixed together, then
cooked in olive oil in a frying
pan to make a crisp thick
pancake.

Cook pasta in a large, deep saucepan of
water: the general rule is 4 cups/1 litre/
1³/4 pt water to 100 g/3¹/2 oz pasta. Bring
water to a rolling boil, toss in salt to taste
(in Italy, 1 tablespoon per every 100 g/
3¹/2 oz pasta is usual), then stir in pasta. If
you wish, add some oil. When water
comes back to the boil, begin timing.
The pasta is done when it is 'al dente',
that is tender but with resistance to the
bite. Remove pasta from water by
straining through a colander or lifting out
of saucepan with tongs or fork.

HOW MUCH TO COOK PER SERVE		
Pasta Type	First Course	Main Meal
Dried pasta	60-75 g	75-100 g
	2-2¹/2 oz	2¹/2-3¹/2 oz
Fresh pasta	75-100 g	125-155 g
	2¹/2-3¹/2 oz	4-5 oz
Filled pasta	155-185 g	185-200 g
(such as ravioli)	5-6 oz	6-6¹/2 oz

PORK AND SAGE FILLED RAVIOLI

1 quantity Homemade Pasta
dough (see recipe)
grated fresh Parmesan cheese

PORK AND SAGE FILLING
315 g/10 oz ricotta cheese, drained
60 g/2 oz lean bacon, finely chopped
155 g/5 oz lean cooked pork, finely
diced
1 teaspoon finely chopped fresh parsley
$^1/_2$ teaspoon finely chopped fresh sage
1 teaspoon grated fresh Parmesan cheese
grated nutmeg
freshly ground black pepper

To make filling, place ricotta cheese, bacon, pork, parsley, sage and Parmesan cheese in a bowl. Mix to combine and season to taste with nutmeg and black pepper. Cover and set aside while making pasta. Assemble, following directions for making ravioli.

Round ravioli can be made by cutting circles from the filled sheets of pasta.

Pork and Sage Filled Ravioli

MAKING RAVIOLI

1 On a lightly floured surface, roll pasta dough to 2 mm/^{1}/16 in thickness and cut into strips. Place strips on a teatowel or floured surface and cover with a damp cloth. Keep dough that is not being used covered.

2 Place small mounds of filling at 4 cm/ 1^1/2 in intervals along a strip of dough, then lay a second strip over the top.

3 Press dough down firmly between the mounds of filling to join the pasta. Using a zigzag pastry wheel cut the ravioli. Place prepared ravioli on a teatowel to dry for 30 minutes.

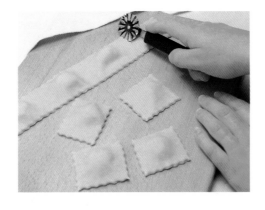

4 Cook ravioli a few at a time in boiling water in a large saucepan for 4 minutes or until 'al dente'. Drain, set aside and keep warm. Sprinkle with Parmesan cheese and serve immediately.

Half Moon Ravioli can be made by cutting the pasta dough into 5 cm/2 in circles. A small amount of filling is then placed in the middle of the circle. The circle is then folded over and the edges pressed firmly together. Dry and cook as for ravioli.

Serves 6

MAKING TORTELLINI

Cut 5 cm/2 in circles of pasta dough. Place a small amount of filling slightly to one side of the middle. Fold over circle so that it falls just short of the other side. Press edges firmly together, curve the semicircle round then pinch the edges together. Dry and cook as for ravioli.

MAKING CAPELLETTI

Remember when making filled pasta to place it, well spaced, on a teatowel to dry for 30 minutes.

Cut 5 cm/2 in squares of pasta. Place a small amount of filling in the centre of each square, then fold in half diagonally to form a triangle, leaving a slight overlap between edges. Press firmly to seal. Wrap the long side of the triangle round a finger until the two ends overlap. Press ends firmly together with the point of the triangle upright. Dry and cook as for ravioli.

CUTTING PASTA BY HAND

Before cutting, roll the pasta dough to the required thickness. For pastas such as tagliatelle, spaghetti, fettuccine and lasagne, roll dough to a 3-5 mm/^{1}/$_8$-^{1}/$_4$ in thickness. For stuffed pasta, such as ravioli and tortellini, roll dough to a 2 mm/^{1}/$_{16}$ in thickness. Any leftover pasta trimmings can be cut into pretty shapes using a biscuit cutter; these make a wonderful garnish for soups.

TAGLIATELLE

Roll pasta dough to 3-5 mm/^{1}/$_8$-^{1}/$_4$ in thickness and cut into wide strips. Roll strips up loosely to form a cylinder and cut into even widths. Shake out pasta into loose nests.

Always cook pasta while making the sauce, so it can be added while it is still hot.

LASAGNE AND CANNELLONI

Roll pasta dough to 3-5 mm/^{1}/$_8$-^{1}/$_4$ in thickness. For lasagne sheets, cut pasta to whatever size will fit your dish. A convenient size is 10 x 12 cm/4 x 5 in. For cannelloni, cut pasta into 10 x 12 cm/4 x 5 in pieces. The cannelloni can then be cooked, filled with a stuffing and rolled before baking.

PAPPARDELLE AND FARFALLE

Roll pasta dough to a 3-5 mm/^{1}/$_8$-^{1}/$_4$ in thickness. To make pappardelle, using a zigzag pastry wheel cut dough into strips 2 cm/^{3}/$_4$ in wide and 30 cm/12 in long. For farfalle, using a pastry wheel cut pasta into 5 cm/2 in squares, then pinch together the middle of each square to give a bow effect.

A large sharp knife is a must when cutting pasta by hand.

TYPES OF PASTA

Convenience of handling and storage, texture and flavour, and good cooking properties will all contribute to the type of pasta that you choose to buy and use. The following guide will help you identify and choose the best type of pasta for you.

Packaged dried pasta: Pasta asciutto comes imported or locally made. It is made from durum wheat semolina and water – labelled 'pasta di semolina di grana duro' in Italian. Eggs are sometimes used, in which case this is marked on the packet – 'all'uovo' on imported brands. Dried pasta requires rehydration as well as cooking, so requires a longer cooking time than fresh pasta.

Commercial fresh pasta: Pasta fresca, is soft and pliable and is usually sold loose. It has the combined flavours of durum wheat, semolina and eggs. Being fresh, it needs only a few minutes cooking time. Although fresh pasta keeps for only 3-5 days, it freezes well and can be kept frozen for several months. To freeze, simply divide it into serving portions, place in freezer bags, seal, label and freeze. When cooking from frozen the pasta only needs to be partially defrosted.

Prepackaged dry 'fresh' pasta: This pasta is made of eggs and should also be made from durum wheat semolina and labelled accordingly.

Pasta, in its simplest form, is a boiled dough of flour and water. In some form or other it has been a staple food of many early civilisations. In Italian, the word 'pasta' means 'dough'.

'On imported brands of pasta, "all'uovo" means that the pasta is made with eggs.'

KEY TO PASTA

1 LASAGNE: These flat sheets of pasta are most often layered with meat, fish or vegetable sauces, topped with cheese, then baked to make a delicious and satisfying dish.

2 PAPPARDELLE: This very wide ribbon pasta was traditionally served with a sauce made of hare, herbs and wine, but today it is teamed with any rich sauce.

3 FETTUCCINE: A flat ribbon pasta that is used in similar ways to spaghetti. Usually sold coiled in nests, fettuccine is particularly good with creamy sauces, which cling better than heavier sauces.

4 TAGLIATELLE: Another of the flat ribbon pastas, tagliatelle is eaten more in the north of Italy than the south and is used in the same ways as fettuccine.

5 SPAGHETTI: Deriving its name from the Italian word 'spago', meaning 'string', spaghetti is the most popular and best known of all pastas outside of Italy. It can be simply served with butter or oil and is good with almost any sauce.

6 SPAGHETTINI: This very thin spaghetti (also known as fedelini) is traditionally served with fish and shellfish sauces, but is equally as delicious served with a tomato sauce.

7 VERMICELLI: This is what the Neapolitans call spaghetti. It comes in many varieties, with very thin vermicelli being sold in clusters, and is ideal for serving with very light sauces. The longer, thicker vermicelli is served in the same way as spaghetti.

8 MACARONI: Short-cut or 'elbow' macaroni, very common outside of Italy, is most often used in baked dishes and in the ever-popular macaroni cheese.

If a suffix is added it indicates:
-ini, a smaller version;
-oni, a larger version;
-rigate, ridged; and
-lisce, smooth.

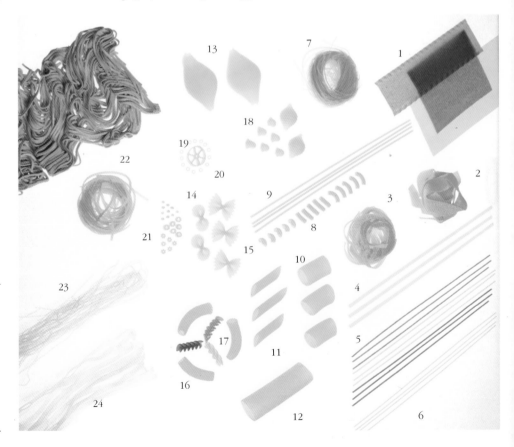

Pasta comes in an array of shapes and sizes, which can sometimes be confusing. However, many shapes are interchangeable and half the appeal of pasta is in inventing your own combinations of pasta and sauce.

9 BUCATINI: This Italian macaroni is usually long like spaghetti, but thicker and hollow. Bucatini is used in the same way as macaroni.

10 RIGATONI: The ridges of this macaroni help sauces cling to it. It comes in many different types and is most often used in baked dishes. Rigatoni can also be stuffed and baked.

11 PENNE: A short tubular pasta, similar to macaroni but with ends cut at an angle rather than straight. It is particularly suited to being served with meat and heavier sauces, which catch in the hollows.

12 CANNELLONI: This large hollow pasta is most often stuffed, topped with a sauce and cheese then baked. Cannelloni can also be stuffed and deep-fried until crisp. If deep-frying, the cannelloni tubes will need to be boiled before stuffing and frying. Flat lasagne noodles can also be used for baked cannelloni; spread the filling down the centre of the pasta before rolling up.

13 CONCHIGLIE: A large, shell-shaped pasta ideal for stuffing. A fish filling is often favoured because of its shape. Conchiglie is often ust referred to as a shell pasta. Small shells, or conchigliette, are used in casseroles, soups and salads.

14 FIOCHETTI: This bow-shaped pasta is ideal for serving with meat and vegetable sauces, as the sauce becomes trapped in the folds.

15 FARFALLE: Meaning 'butterflies', farfelle is used in the same way as fiochetti.

16 FUSILLI: A hollow, spiral-shaped pasta that is great served with substantial meat sauces, as the sauce becomes trapped in the coils or twists.

17 TORTIGLIONI: Another spiral-shaped pasta that is used in the same way as fusilli.

18 LUMACHE: Taking its name from the Italian word for 'snail', this pasta resembles short macaroni but is larger, with a curve at one end. It is used in similar ways to conchigliette.

19 ROTELLI: This wheel-shaped pasta is added to savoury bakes, salads and soups.

20 ANELLI: Small rings of pasta usually used in soups.

21 PASTINA: There are numerous small pasta, such as anellini, ditalini and stellini. They are mostly added to soups.

22 EGG NOODLES: These flat Oriental noodles are often used in soups, while the round noodles are served with sauces and are best for stir-fries. They are also served as an accompaniment, instead of rice.

23 RICE NOODLES: Made from rice flour these noodles are served with spicy sauces and used in soups and stir-fry dishes.

24 TRANSPARENT NOODLES: Also called cellophane noodles, these noodles are added to Oriental soups and deep-fried as a garnish.

Durum wheat used in commercial pasta-making is a species of 'hard' wheat, so called because it has an endosperm rich in gluten. It has a distinctive nutty flavour and a rich amber colour. When milled to a coarsely ground meal – known as semolina – and mixed with water, the resulting dough has the characteristics ideal for commercial pasta-making.

Regional cooking traditions should not be ignored, but there are some general rules that will ensure you enjoy your pasta to the fullest: thin, long pasta needs a good clinging sauce; hollow or twisted shapes take chunky sauces; wide, flat noodles carry rich sauces; and delicate shapes require a light sauce without large pieces in it.

'The flour used for commercial pasta is made from a "hard" wheat called durum wheat.'

USEFUL INFORMATION

QUICK CONVERTER

Metric	Imperial
5 mm	$1/4$ in
1 cm	$1/2$ in
2 cm	$3/4$ in
2.5 cm	1 in
5 cm	2 in
10 cm	4 in
15 cm	6 in
20 cm	8 in
23 cm	9 in
25 cm	10 in
30 cm	12 in

MEASURING LIQUIDS

Metric	Imperial	Cup
30 mL	1 fl oz	
60 mL	2 fl oz	$1/4$ cup
90 mL	3 fl oz	
125 mL	4 fl oz	$1/2$ cup
155 mL	5 fl oz	
170 mL	$5 1/2$ fl oz	$2/3$ cup
185 mL	6 fl oz	
220 mL	7 fl oz	
250 mL	8 fl oz	1 cup
500 mL	16 fl oz	2 cups
600 mL	20 fl oz (1 pt)	
750 mL	$1 1/4$ pt	
1 litre	$1 3/4$ pt	4 cups
1.2 litres	2 pt	

METRIC CUPS & SPOONS

Metric	Cups	Imperial
60 mL	$1/4$ cup	2 fl oz
80 mL	$1/3$ cup	$2 1/2$ fl oz
125 mL	$1/2$ cup	4 fl oz
250 mL	1 cup	8 fl oz
	Spoons	
1.25 mL	$1/4$ teaspoon	
2.5 mL	$1/2$ teaspoon	
5 mL	1 teaspoon	
20 mL	1 tablespoon	

MEASURING DRY INGREDIENTS

Metric	Imperial
15 g	$1/2$ oz
30 g	1 oz
60 g	2 oz
90 g	3 oz
125 g	4 oz
155 g	5 oz
185 g	6 oz
220 g	7 oz
250 g	8 oz
280 g	9 oz
315 g	10 oz
375 g	12 oz
410 g	13 oz
440 g	14 oz
470 g	15 oz
500 g	16 oz (1 lb)
750 g	1 lb 8 oz
1 kg	2 lb
1.5 kg	3 lb

OVEN TEMPERATURES

°C	°F	Gas Mark
120	250	$1/2$
140	275	1
150	300	2
160	325	3
180	350	4
190	375	5
200	400	6
220	425	7
240	475	8
250	500	9

In this book, ingredients such as fish and meat are given in grams so you know how much to buy. It is handy to have:
- A small inexpensive set of kitchen scales

Other ingredients in our recipes are given in tablespoons and cups, so you will need:
- A nest of measuring cups (1 cup, $1/2$ cup, $1/3$ cup and $1/4$ cup)
- A set of measuring spoons (1 tablespoon, 1 teaspoon, $1/2$ teaspoon and $1/4$ teaspoon)
- A transparent graduated measuring jug (1 litre or 250 mL) for measuring liquids
- Cup and spoon measures are level

INDEX